Regenerating Cities

LEADERSHIP · VISION · PARTNERSHIPS

EDITED BY

WAHEED NAZIR
RICHARD COWELL

Published by Outstanding Books
Lichfield House
35 Lichfield Road
Birmingham B5 6RW

publish@outstandingbooks.co.uk
www.outstandingbooks.co.uk

Cover Design by Zain (Faadil)
Typeset in the United Kingdom by OUTSTANDING

CONTENTS

ACKNOWLEDGEMENTS

WAHEED NAZIR

I would like to thank all the authors for their brilliant contributions to this book. All of you have taken time away from your families and friends to accommodate this in your busy schedules, and for this, I am sincerely grateful.

I have been fortunate to have worked alongside many of you over the years, and a number of you have been firm friends of mine long before we embarked on this particular journey. Each of you have truly inspired me with your passion and energy to deliver change on a transformational scale.

I would like to give a special mention to Sir Edward Lister and Tony Pidgley CBE. It was the both of you who inspired me to undertake this endeavour, to capture the collective experience, knowledge and unique insight of leading figures in this sector, with the aim to inspire future generations. Tony, in particular, has given me tremendous support throughout this process. I will always be indebted to him for his advice and motivating me to bring the concept of this book into reality.

The process of writing my own chapter, alongside co-editing this book, has been more challenging than I first imagined. Richard Cowell, who agreed to co-edit with me, has provided immense dedication to the whole project. I have no doubt it would have taken years to pull together had it not been for his instrumental input. I know that he is enormously appreciative of his family's loving support and patience.

I would also like to thank Rob Bartlett for reviewing my chapter and whose guidance has been invaluable, Imran Majid for his sterling research work, Uyen-Phan Han for her meticulous proof reading, and Johnny Killock who sourced the wonderful images and addressed copyright issues.

Louise O'Neill has been an integral part of the book's production and has sacrificed her personal time; working weekends and late into the night to see the project through to completion. Without Louise's untiring assistance, this book would not have been possible.

I owe infinite gratitude to my wife, and our children, Aisha and Muhammed. Your love, patience and support sustain me. I am sure you did not anticipate how many weekends would be lost when I first mentioned my intention to do this, but I promise I shall make it up to you. And finally, to my parents: loving thanks – you have instilled in me, that with hard work and commitment, anything is possible. I will be forever grateful to you both for your belief in me and for your lifelong support and encouragement.

INTRODUCTION

RICHARD COWELL

It is widely acknowledged that urbanisation as a global mega trend is set to continue. As the world's population grows, and more people are attracted to live in cities either through necessity or desire, so too does the need for cities to keep pace providing the facilities and amenities to meet demand. Coupled with environmental, economic and societal challenges, cities need to evolve and adapt at an ever greater pace.

Successful cities are responding to these challenges and taking the opportunities that are presented to them.

In the UK, regional cities are emerging from a period of economic decline that had seen the collapse of traditional industries, decreasing populations, degraded environments and desperately poor reputations. By reimaging their role many of these cities are now defining a new future in the 21st Century.

They are fast becoming hubs for cultural and civic activity; drivers of research and innovation, attractive leisure destinations and compelling places to live and work. There is now a strong narrative to the importance of cities and how they contribute to the national economy.

Achieving such change has required a concerted effort from across the public and private sector. The delivery of new homes, offices and industrial premises, and the provision of leisure, cultural and retail facilities have diversified their offer and brought new life to city centres. The provision of new public spaces and significant investment in infrastructure has underpinned the creation of more attractive and accessible destinations. Those cities that are embracing regeneration are finding renewed activity and purpose, resulting in positive changes for their economies.

This regeneration does not however happen over-night nor in a silo. It is happening in the context of ageing infrastructure, stretched budgets and environmental and political imperatives for change. Current and future approaches to regeneration need to ensure that the people who live in the city benefit from the investment. An inclusive approach needs to be coupled with the creation of an environmental legacy and the adoption of more sustainable, resource-efficient ways of managing cities and delivering development.

Securing cities competitiveness is increasingly challenging. The market place is becoming crowded and cities need to utilise their heritage and cultural identity to create compelling narratives for their future.

Delivering homes, infrastructure and jobs requires clear strategy but quick action, not least because decisions are made in real time in the context of a fluid and uncertain world. The established patterns of development and inherited infrastructure present a further factor to which the planning and delivery of regeneration and development must fit and respond. There are very few blank canvases on which to work.

No less important but much harder to quantify are the perceptions of a city. These can be just as important to those looking to invest, live or establish a business. Aligned to this is the need to create relationships and engage with diverse communities. These are as much a part of successful city regeneration as the physical plans and investment.

As a result, bringing forward coherent approaches to regeneration, at the same time as navigating those complexities, is no easy task. The factors that are influencing the approach are broad.

Setting the strategy, creating partnerships, focusing on outcomes and aligning resources are all key. The ability to combine the best of the public and private sector, the delivery of infrastructure and utilisation of new forms of investment to unlock sites are all essential to the reinvention of cities. And while there is no magic formula, successful regeneration can hinge on one key component: strong leadership and vision.

The experience of those who have led regeneration in the UK provides a snapshot of what can be achieved with a core set of values and a commitment to deliver change.

In this book, ten of the UK's most important and inspirational leaders explain how they have approached the challenges and led the delivery of major regeneration. Not only have they instigated change but they have also sustained this regeneration by pioneering creative and innovative approaches.

Spanning the public and private sector, with backgrounds across planning, property, finance and infrastructure, the ten authors give a personal account of their experience and how they have achieved successful outcomes for the cities in which they have worked.

The public sector has a defining role in shaping cities providing the certainty, through clear leadership and strategic direction that investors, developers and communities seek. Waheed Nazir, Corporate Director Economy at Birmingham City Council and Sir Howard Bernstein, Chief Executive of Manchester City Council between 1998 and 2017, provide their perspective on how local government can, through a combination of vision, planning and innovation lead the reinvention of cities.

Aligned to the role of the public sector is that of the development industry, which has a central role in delivering the buildings and spaces where we live, work and spend leisure time. Tony Pidgley CBE, Chairman and Founder of Berkeley Group; Helen Gordon, Chief Executive Officer at Grainger plc; and David Partridge, Managing Partner at Argent set out how they and the companies they lead are delivering high quality regeneration and development schemes.

An essential ingredient to great regeneration is the ability to collaborate and work in partnership. Sir Edward Lister, Chairman of Homes England and former Leader of Wandsworth Borough Council and Dame Alison Nimmo DBE, Chief Executive of The Crown Estate explain how successful partnerships have been integral to making things happen.

The foundation of any city is its social and physical infrastructure. Sir John Armitt CBE, Chairman of the National Infrastructure Commission, National Express Group and City & Guilds Group, sets out how infrastructure, in all its forms, is necessary for cities to grow and prosper.

The confidence of the market and availability of funding is paramount to delivering development and infrastructure. Bill Hughes, Head of Real Assets at Legal & General Investment Management and Marc Mogull, Co-Founder, Executive Chairman and Chief Investment Officer at Benson Elliot Capital describe the challenges and opportunities that exist to unlocking private and institutional investment and securing finance for the development and regeneration of cities.

HOW TO MAKE A GREAT CITY

WAHEED NAZIR

WAHEED NAZIR

Waheed has held senior positions at Birmingham City Council over the last 15 years. His current portfolio includes planning and regeneration, transport and infrastructure, housing development, highways, and a £1.5bn property portfolio.

His strategic approach to economic growth has involved launching major policy initiatives including the Big City Plan and the statutory Birmingham Development Plan, the creation of the country's largest Enterprise Zone, and driving forward multi-billion pound redevelopment schemes including Birmingham Smithfield, HS2 Curzon, Peddimore and Ladywood.

He has led the establishment of a series of commercial vehicles for the City Council including InReach, the Council's Private Rented Sector residential delivery vehicle; an investment vehicle for commercial property development; and Birmingham Municipal Housing Trust, shaping it into one of the UK's largest public sector house builders. He has lead responsibility for delivering the Commonwealth Games 2022 Athletes Village, which includes the direct delivery of a new 1,500 home legacy development.

Waheed is a non-executive Director of Birmingham Airport Holdings Limited and Chairman of Arden Cross Limited, a development vehicle for the 350 acre site located around the Solihull HS2 interchange station.

Waheed is also a visiting Professor at Birmingham City University and in July 2017 he was awarded an honorary Doctorate by Aston University.

Birmingham, like many cities across the globe, has undergone periods of prosperity and times of relative decline. It has evolved from a small 7th Century Anglo-Saxon hamlet at the fringe of the ancient kingdom of Mercia to become a major international city.

In the 12th Century, a local Lord of the Manor, Peter de Birmingham, boldly set out to secure the 1st market charter from Henry II. His reward was to see Birmingham go from a quiet backwater to a key provincial market town, establishing its reputation as a centre for trade and commerce.

By the 18th Century, Birmingham became the cradle of the industrial revolution, known across the globe as the 'City of a Thousand Trades' and the 'Workshop of the World'. A multitude of creative industries made everything from buttons to whistles, machines to jewellery. Its world-class infrastructure of canals and railways shipped those wares to buyers on every continent.

The city reached its peak in the post-war years thanks to the growth of the automotive industry when it became synonymous with cars. And then, slowly but surely, cars became the root cause of the city's decline with the automotive sector being its main industry.

Economies don't stand still. By the 1980's, the globalisation of manufacturing had led to large swathes of industrial activity being outsourced across the world. As the car plants closed, Birmingham was left behind economically and socially.

To its credit, the city recognised the need for change. As early as 1988, the city convened the Highbury Initiative, an international symposium to explore ideas for Birmingham's renewal. The proposals had some major impact in the city. Parts of the city centre were pedestrianised and sections of the inner ring road were moved. The International Convention Centre was launched and Brindleyplace, a major mixed used development, was delivered, helping to regenerate a stretch of the canal network.

The initiative slowed the decline, but did not reverse it. By the late 2000's, it was high time for Birmingham to find a new direction.

In 2009, at the age of 34, I became Director of Planning and Regeneration at Birmingham City Council.

On my first day I recall feeling a huge sense of excitement. I was leading one of the great cities of England and in charge of the largest local planning authority in the country: this would be a fantastic, career-defining role. More importantly, it was an immense honour. Birmingham is my home city. It is where I was born and where I have spent most of my life.

At the same time, I also felt that the agenda was both clear and daunting. The city needed to create homes, diversify its economic base and deliver new infrastructure. More than anything, it needed to change perceptions. The city had to show that it was open for business so that it could attract and sustain new investment, which in turn would bring about the scale of improvements necessary to turn the city's fortunes around.

Most of all, however, I recall the overwhelming sense of opportunity. Yes, Birmingham had seen better days, but it still had one of the youngest, most diverse and fast-growing populations in Europe. I had the chance to shape the future of a city and opportunities like that don't come around often.

A personal challenge

It was undoubtedly going to be a huge challenge for the city to reach its full potential, but the task felt very personal to me.

I grew up in Birmingham's eastern neighbourhoods. As a kid I recall looking forward to every weekend when the whole family would go to the Bull Ring markets; my brother, two sisters and I would spend hours running around the stalls. It was a diverse area with a real sense of community; a place where people of all backgrounds would mix freely in the heart of the city. I remember we would spend the whole day shopping and eating, meeting new people and learning about different cultures.

But however engaged I was in our local community, I was certainly not engaged at school. A lack of interest in studying meant I did not pass even one GCSE.

My father has always been an inspiration to me and our conversation after receiving my results was a turning point. He gave me a choice: either work seven days a week, 52 weeks a year in one of his businesses, or go back, start again, and get a real education. His message was clear: reach for the stars and, whatever you choose to do in life, give it everything you can.

Thinking back on that choice now, I recognise that beneath my fond childhood memories, my working-class neighbourhood had been challenged by the symptoms of economic decline, social exclusion, poor health and low attainment in education. I decided to go back to studying.

A few years later, I graduated with a first class honours degree in urban planning and development from the University of Westminster, London.

My family undoubtedly provided the greatest motivation for that turnaround. We all have a responsibility to leave a legacy for those that follow. I wanted to deliver the sort of place that my parents could grow old in and that my children would be proud to say their dad helped to shape. I wanted to create places that would help people to thrive, driven by an awareness of how close I came to wasting my own potential.

Work to do...

On that first morning in 2009, there were some very real and immediate challenges to tackle.

The first was to continue to remove the physical barriers that divided the city. Birmingham had not only developed a reputation for building cars, it had been rebuilt for the car and the road network had choked the life out of the city centre.

Modern economies need to be built on a diverse base. Cities and institutions need to foster knowledge, creativity and connections to thrive. In architectural terms they need to be permeable, with a mix of uses connected by public spaces that create opportunities for different people to meet and interact. The design of our cities need to encourage the personal relationships, social interactions and, ultimately, the creative ideas that drive a knowledge-intensive economy.

Many of the world's most exciting cities have been reshaped in this way. Melbourne is known for its arcades and walkways that incubate the dynamism and vibrancy of its diverse population. Its architecture has undoubtedly helped to make it the cultural capital of Australia. London's tightly packed warren of alleys, courts and squares encourages people to wander, meet, encounter new ideas, and develop the productive relationships that are essential for business success.

Perhaps the best example of all is Barcelona. Wander down Las Ramblas and notice how cars are nowhere to be seen. Instead, the markets spill out into the pedestrianised street and the buildings are a mix of restaurants, shops, offices and flats. The architecture and planning amplifies every social interaction, giving the city an excitement and energy that few places can match and that attracts visitors and investment from around the world.

The second big challenge we faced was bureaucracy.

Birmingham's extraordinary success in the 18th and 19th Centuries was driven by collaboration between the city's industrialists and strong civic leaders. The likes of Joseph Chamberlain, Mayor of Birmingham, and his son Neville Chamberlain, who was Lord Mayor of Birmingham and later the British Prime Minister, were leaders who could both see the big picture and make change happen. They were instrumental in shaping the civic and social institutions that made the city renowned across the world.

By contrast, at the turn of this Century, the way the city operated held it back. Public organisations and council departments were fiercely independent, skills were siloed and innovation was stifled.

But the third and most important challenge that we faced on that first morning in 2009 was a lack of clarity over what the city wanted to achieve.

I have often thought that in any walk of life you can deliver a hundred different initiatives and make little difference, whereas focusing on four or five key strategic interventions can be transformational. At the outset we had no clear vision of what those priorities should be. We needed to develop a plan to make the city great again.

How to make a great city

To my mind there are five key elements which help make a great city:

1   Strong vision and civic leadership;

2   A focus on clear outcomes;

3   Ensuring delivery through effective partnerships;

4   An innovative culture based on multi-disciplinary teams; and

5   Resilience through diversity.

It is evident to me that the great modern cities around the world have put these principles into action.

First and foremost, dynamic global cities like Melbourne, Barcelona, London, Chicago and Madrid have all benefitted from civic and business leaders coming together to create a shared vision for the place they want to live and work in. They have codified that shared vision in flexible urban masterplans that serve as frameworks to guide development. These plans are responsive to market demands and create compelling environments for people by building on the city's competitive strengths, unique character and local heritage.

Secondly, those great cities have remained focused on what they need to achieve rather than getting lost in the minutiae of how to achieve it. Planning and economic decisions will always provoke heated debate. Land is a finite resource and competition for its use is intense. Prioritising strategic objectives rather than getting bogged down in the details of planning processes has enabled those cities to achieve amazing results.

Thirdly, to deliver on their vision, civic leaders have had to build relationships and forge partnerships between different interest groups. I have always been struck by the importance of working with others to find a common understanding in order to make change happen. Effective and trusting relationships between the private sector, local and national government, and affected communities are essential to enable the level of innovation required to solve the complex, multi-faceted problems faced by all cities.

Fourthly, enabling cities to grow requires a great degree of skill, and so cities that excel at urban planning typically have multidisciplinary teams which align all the key decision-makers to focus on delivering place-making. Forming these teams and fostering a culture that enables innovation, risk and creativity is essential.

The fifth and final attribute of great cities is diversity. In any dense urban environment creating places that facilitate people coming together is key, be that through enhanced connectivity, mixing uses or creating spaces for interaction. Without that diversity, the economic base is more exposed to economic disruption and the social bonds of a place are weakened.

In particular, as living standards rise, access to affordable housing is critical to meet the needs of residents in the city and to ensure that they are not displaced as the city grows in prosperity. Put simply, great cities are diverse places and diversity creates resilience in the face of economic and social change.

Of course Birmingham is not Madrid. It is not Melbourne or Chicago or London. The real battle was not just to learn from others but to apply that knowledge in our local context.

Vision

First and foremost, we had to develop our vision for Birmingham. Fortunately, I took over after the departure of Clive Dutton OBE. He was a great visionary, a close friend and a wonderful individual whose early work was instrumental in Birmingham's subsequent transformation. I always look back on the time I spent with him as hugely important.

Birmingham needed both a vision and, just as importantly, a means to communicate it effectively. The city needed a symbol that everyone could rally around and that would set out how we would create a shared future. We took that idea forward to develop the Big City Plan for Birmingham, which was first published in 2010. The Big City Plan defined a clear vision for the growth of the city in terms that were bold, flexible but also simple.

Creating it was a difficult task. On the one hand, we had to develop a sound understanding of the evidence base for where the city's competitive advantages lay. On the other hand, we had to focus on the big picture, and the key strategic interventions that would allow us to transform the place.

The Big City Plan not only crystallised our vision for Birmingham's future it provided a roadmap for delivering its regeneration. The evidence over the past 10 years shows that it has stood the test of time. During my term as Director, I have worked with four different council leaders, seen a change in ruling party and served four different chief executives. The vision set out in the Big City Plan has remained constant throughout the changing political context.

Focus on outcomes

Key to the success of the Big City Plan was that it set about defining guiding principles, rather than acting as a rigid planning document bound by rules and regulations.

We needed the Plan to be flexible because of the lengthy timescales involved in realising urban transformation, enabling it to influence investment further down the line. It had to be able to evolve with the city while keeping everyone involved focused on making progress toward the long-term outcomes we wanted to achieve.

In the early stages of the process, my team and I discussed whether we should prepare a statutory plan for the city centre. We concluded that this approach would be too time consuming and inflexible, at odds with the vision we wanted to pursue, and impede the creation of a vibrant and dynamic city centre.

A focus on process rather than outcomes is still a major issue for the built environment profession and undermines the ability to deliver better places across the UK. Producing a technically sound report or meeting certain legally prescribed tests will not guarantee the delivery of a successful place. Delivery of the desired outcomes is, therefore, where the real challenges lie.

The launch of the Big City Plan was the turning point when we became bold enough to take control of our destiny by focusing solely on tangible outcomes and leaving bureaucratic processes to one side.

Our ambition was to bring energy and vibrancy back to the city's core, in part by encouraging densification. We would break through the city's physical barriers, while also giving people a reason to come into the centre by creating new public spaces and championing the cultural institutions that would make it a place where residents and visitors wanted to spend their leisure time.

But that vision would count for nothing if it could not be delivered. We also needed objective yardsticks against which to judge our results. As a team, we needed to be accountable to the people and their elected leaders.

The targets we set were to grow the centre by 25%, creating 15,000 new homes and 50,000 new jobs. Why those numbers? Because they were big. They signalled ambition in the clearest possible terms, at a time when most outsiders would have said ambition was something Birmingham had conspicuously lacked.

But make no mistake, while the ambition and strategy were based on clear evidence as to the city's competitive strengths, the targets we set were based on judgment, not data. That might surprise some people but with hindsight, it was absolutely the right approach. We were looking to forge a new future, the data and statistics from Birmingham's recent past only told the story of the city's relative decline. In the absence of a meaningful benchmark, we had to trust our judgment.

In all walks of life, the reality will always be that we live in a world of imperfect information. To achieve a step-change in approach – as a person, as a company, as a city or as a society – will always require a leap of faith. It will always require self-belief that you can change the patterns of the past. At the time, while some undoubtedly saw that scale of ambition as a high risk strategy, in truth we felt we had no other choice.

Ensuring delivery through effective partnerships

In the early 2010's, the UK was only just emerging from the greatest economic crisis of a generation. The recession of 2008 had put unprecedented strain on public finances. Birmingham's grant from central government was slashed and our own revenue from local taxation was limited.

If we wanted to fundamentally transform the city, we had to be innovative. More specifically, we had to form partnerships with the private sector, central government and local communities. We knew we did not have the resources to act alone, but we were not prepared to use the straitened times as an excuse for inaction.

In 2011, with the Big City Plan in place, we used our ambitious growth targets to secure an Enterprise Zone (EZ) together with our Local Enterprise Partnership. Thanks to the EZ, we were allowed to retain 100% of the growth in local business rates for 25 years, providing us with additional revenue to fund infrastructure improvements. We took inspiration from the United States, specifically the idea of Tax Incremental Financing Initiatives (TIFs). TIFs use the projected local tax generated from investment and development as security to borrow against, allowing authorities to fund up-front infrastructure requirements to enable development and growth.

We began to fund development sites which required infrastructure to become viable. The investment in public transport, cycling, public realm, education and training has been integral to the city's approach to growth. Today the EZ gives us access to over £2 billion to invest into infrastructure.

Even with new funding available thanks to the EZ, it was still critical to bring in private sector partners, if we were to meet our targets. To deliver the homes, employment space and mix of uses that the city centre needed in order to flourish, we needed new sources of both capital and skills.

Our partners needed to share our ambition to drive the renaissance of the city and understand our priorities. Within the Big City Plan we had identified five strategic growth areas that we needed to unlock if we were to achieve our vision for the city centre. The first of those was Birmingham's principal train station, New Street.

If you visited Birmingham prior to the transformation of New Street Station you will know that as a welcome to the city it was poor. As a rail passenger, the experience was barely tolerable. Its redevelopment, completed in 2015, was a turning point for Birmingham and only possible because of the partnership with Network Rail and investment from Government with over £600 million. The new station not only opened up physical access to the city centre and improved the experience for rail passengers, it also redefined perceptions of Birmingham.

The vision attracted John Lewis to invest in an anchor retail store as the centrepiece of a larger mixed-use development above the station, known as Grand Central. Partnering with John Lewis to anchor the scheme not only delivered a significant financial contribution to a strategic redevelopment of the city centre, it also acted as a major vote of confidence in Birmingham. It made the market sit up and take notice.

Another of the priority areas in the Big City Plan centred on Paradise, which was key to removing the physical barrier to reconnect the city centre core to the westside of the city. It was also critical to further diversify the city's financial and professional services offer. The case study is summarised on page 22.

NEW STREET STATION BEFORE DEVELOPMENT

NEW STREET STATION AFTER REDEVELOPMENT

Paradise development – case study

SIZE AND SCALE	£700 million GDV, over 160,000 sq.m. floorspace across 7 hectare (ha) site.
USES	Grade A office space in 8 buildings, leisure and food & beverage at ground floor and a hotel.
INFRASTRUCTURE	Three new public squares, reconfigured highways and new pedestrian routes.
PARTNERS	Corporate Joint Venture between Birmingham City Council (landowner) and BTPS and Hermes (investor partners) with Argent (development management services for each phase). The Enterprise Zone provided infrastructure funding to unlock the site.
TIMESCALES	Three phased development that commenced in 2015; first phase complete 2019 with phase 2 due to complete 2022. Final phase due to commence 2023.
IMPACTS	Over 10,000 jobs; £500m of net additional GVA per annum; and significant improvements to pedestrian permeability and public realm.
LOCATION	Sitting at the intersection between the city centre core which includes the civic heart and the central business district; the Jewellery Quarter and the Westside area.
HISTORY OF THE SITE	The site formed part of the overall Manzoni Plan for the redevelopment of Birmingham after the Second World War. Paradise Circus, in its original form, was masterplanned by John Madin and opened in the 1970s as a mixed retail area with the principal building being the Central Library. In its original form Paradise Circus created a major barrier between the City Centre Core and surrounding areas including the location of the International Convention Centre, Brindleyplace and Broad Street.
THE STRATEGY	Identified in the Big City Plan (2010) as one of the five areas of transformation to grow the city centre. The strategy for the site focused on expanding the business district by breaking the concrete collar and removing the dysfunctional group of buildings and subways that formed Paradise Circus. The site is part of the Enterprise Zone.
CHALLENGES TO DELIVERY	The development was unviable without Enterprise Zone funding due to the scale of infrastructure and site reconfiguration required. The project reshaped the highway network and had to maintain the operation of the A38 tunnel. The Central Library and Birmingham Conservatoire needed relocating. The site is adjacent to the civic heart of the city with its Grade I and II* Listed Buildings.

PARADISE CIRCUS BEFORE DEVELOPMENT

PROPOSED PARADISE DEVELOPMENT

The single most significant proposal in the Big City Plan, which was also very personal to me, is Smithfield, the area where Birmingham's original markets were founded. Putting aside my childhood nostalgia, the sprawling 1970s wholesale market complex had become a barrier to, rather than a conduit for, social interactions. It blocked off historic neighbourhoods like Digbeth and the Chinese Quarter from the centre, isolating them from the city's social, economic and political life.

Breaking through this barrier was central to our vision for the city. We knew that the scale of the markets would make for a complex project. More importantly, we recognised that the community needed to support the vision if it was to be successful. Over 100 traders operated from those market stalls; we needed both to find a more suitable site and convince the traders of the benefits of moving. We needed to work with them as a core partner throughout that process.

It is still many years before it is complete, but this £1.8 billion project is the one that will have the greatest positive impact on the city. It will reposition the city on the international stage by creating spaces for communities to come together celebrating Birmingham's past, present and future. To see the markets that were such a central part of my childhood being transformed for a new generation has been one of the proudest achievements of my tenure. The case study is summarised on page 26.

CHURCH OF ST MARTIN IN THE BULL RING LEADING DOWN TO
THE SITE OF BIRMINGHAM SMITHFIELD, TAKEN IN 1880'S

BIRMINGHAM'S RETAIL MARKETS IN THE 1800'S

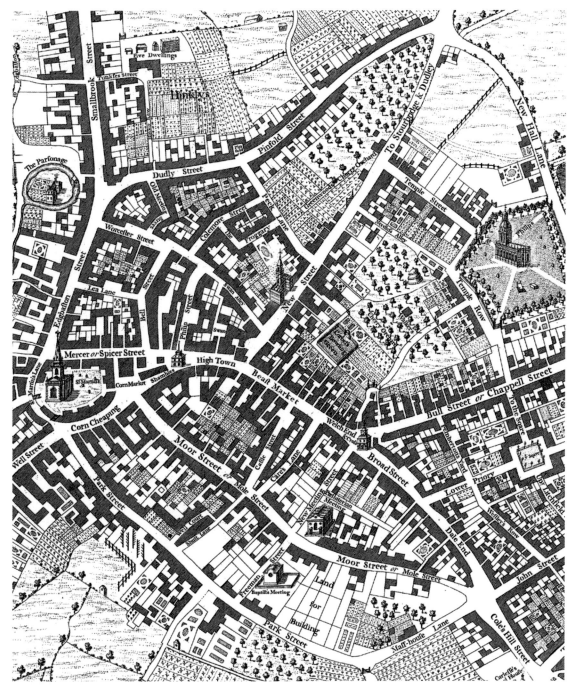

PLAN OF BIRMINGHAM CITY CENTRE: SURVEYED IN THE YEAR 1731

Birmingham Smithfield development – case study

SIZE AND SCALE	£1.8 billion GDV, set over 500,000 sq.m. of floorspace across 17 hectare (ha) site.
USES	A mixed-use family destination with a unique leisure and cultural offer; incorporating new retail markets and including space for independent retailers and small businesses. The scheme also includes over 2,000 new homes.
INFRASTRUCTURE	Over 4.3 hectares of new high-quality public realm space, including a community park and civic square. New transport links include metro and bus interchange, a school and other supporting community facilities.
PARTNERS	Contractual Joint Venture between Birmingham City Council (landowner and promoter) and Lendlease (delivery and investment partner).
TIMESCALES	15 year development with first phase of the scheme anticipated to start 2022.
IMPACTS	Over 8,000 jobs; £230m of net additional GVA per annum. The scheme will also deliver significant social value including apprenticeships, volunteering opportunities, additional support for community organisations and projects, funding for social enterprises and the local business supply chain.
LOCATION	In the heart of the city centre, adjoining the Bullring shopping centre, Chinese Quarter, Digbeth creative district and New Street Station. Smithfield is also a short walk from the site of the new High Speed 2 city centre terminus station.
HISTORY OF THE SITE	Birmingham's first markets were held at Smithfield over 800 years ago; it is the birthplace of the city's rich history as a centre of trade, commerce and innovation.
THE STRATEGY	Smithfield was identified in the Big City Plan (2010) as one of five areas of transformation to enable the growth of the city centre. The site is part of the Enterprise Zone and is being developed according to a masterplan produced by the city council in 2016.
CHALLENGES TO DELIVERY	The masterplan required the relocation of the wholesale markets. A new facility opened at the Food Hub, Witton in 2018 safeguarding over 100 businesses and 600 jobs. The redevelopment of the site requires a Compulsory Purchase Order (CPO), the closure of key roads, demolition and utility diversions.
PROCUREMENT PROCESS	OJEU compliant via competitive dialogue with 80% of the weighting assigned to quality, including social value, environmental sustainability and place making.

BIRMINGHAM SMITHFIELD - SITE IN 2018 WITH FORMER WHOLESALE MARKETS IN SITU

BIRMINGHAM SMITHFIELD – PROPOSED DEVELOPMENT   PHOTO COURTESY OF LENDLEASE

Innovative culture and multi-disciplinary teams

At the outset I knew that these ambitious projects could only be delivered by a committed and talented team. Yet my early years in office were marked by upheaval within the council.

In the straitened fiscal climate following the 2008 recession, we had no choice but to downsize. But I was determined that we should emerge leaner and more effective from the restructuring. We managed to keep some brilliant staff and organised them into multi-disciplinary teams focused on specific geographic areas. We also made a conscious effort to give them autonomy, trusting them to do the right thing.

This committed and hungry group had a clear understanding of the interplay between housing, jobs and infrastructure, of the value of place-making and harnessing the DNA of the city to drive its future growth. As a result, productivity shot up. Following the restructuring the team proved more effective than it had ever been before, despite having 30% fewer people.

Integrating our staff into multi-disciplinary teams allowed us to become more customer-focused. We could make clear decisions that offered certainty to everyone, from individual homeowners wanting an extension to major developers considering multi-million pound investments.

The truth is that while delivering the major transformation projects is hugely rewarding, those successes always depend on being able to deal with the details. Delivering business as usual in an efficient and effective way is where you can make an instant tangible difference for customers, residents and partners.

Ensuring timely decisions on planning permissions and infrastructure plans fosters confidence. Over the long term, it gives people the conviction to continue to invest in more ambitious projects, as you demonstrate the organisational competence to deliver on the promises you make. Collaboration then fosters innovation in a virtuous circle.

Sustaining this culture is a continual challenge in the face of ongoing financial pressures and skills shortages across the built environment profession. To ensure a pipeline of new talent, Birmingham Council now runs one of the largest graduate schemes in the country. Senior members of the department are committed to lecturing on university courses and mentoring young professionals.

My staff continue to inspire me every day with their ability to anticipate the challenges of tomorrow as well as meeting the challenges of today. Their passion and commitment fills me with confidence that whatever momentum we can build for the city now, will be maintained for many years to come.

Resilience through diversity

Our approach in Birmingham is driven by a desire to create places that will be resilient in the face of long-term economic and social change. This has influenced every aspect of decision-making. At a practical level, we wanted to increase diversity within the economic base by ensuring provision of a sufficient range and supply of employment land; create sustainable neighbourhoods characterised by a wide choice of housing sizes, types and tenures; promote diversity of uses within our urban centres; and create places that are distinctive, well-designed and sustainable, making the most effective use of land.

Beyond the city centre and the Big City Plan we knew that we had to ensure that sufficient land was released from the green belt to enable communities to be created at a scale that would be sustainable. Urban extensions need to include schools, healthcare, sport and recreation facilities, alongside a mix of housing types and tenures and commercial, retail and leisure uses, if they are to become established as sustainable desirable neighbourhoods.

More specifically, our desire to foster long-term resilience led to a focus on social diversity within the city. We have been acutely conscious of the risk of regeneration equating to gentrification of city neighbourhoods. If development drives away the very young or the old, the students, the teachers, nurses and artists, then the fruits of prosperity are ultimately wasted; the city loses valuable skills and leaves itself vulnerable in the face of future economic and social shocks.

The emphasis on inclusion and serving broad society may sound radical or overly political to some. Given my personal background in a working-class immigrant neighbourhood, I cannot claim to be wholly objective here.

A commitment to improving the quality of life for rich and poor alike underpinned the modern discipline of Planning as it was developed by the likes of Ebenezer Howard. It was central to the commercial ethos of many of our most famous industrialists, most notably the Cadburys, founders of the famous chocolate company. The neighbourhood they created, Bournville, defined a new form of city living with family housing, public spaces and amenities and set a benchmark for quality development that we are still seeking to replicate today.

I am convinced that the impact on the most disadvantaged in society has to be the ultimate yardstick for judging the success of any planning and economic policy. If even the most disadvantaged are encouraged to thrive, that is the sign of a confident and inclusive place that will be well-placed to adapt as the economic, business and political cycles turn.

Birmingham as an international city

As the development of the city gathered pace through the 2010s, the question began to arise of how to ensure momentum could be maintained in an increasingly challenging global context. How could Birmingham continue to attract inward investment over the long-term, establishing itself as a regional, national and international force?

Our vision and ambition for the city was continuing to evolve. By now we also had a proven track record of delivering major strategic projects. That combination proved critical to winning the right to host the 2022 Commonwealth Games (CWG). One of the challenges within our bid was how to build an Athletes' Village for 6,500 competitors and officials in less than 4 years.

We have been building homes as a developer in the city for almost 10 years but this project would be very different. Creating the Athletes' Village has involved balancing the requirements of the Games, with the long-term needs of the city. On the one hand, the location needed to provide sufficient amenity space for national teams during the event. On the other, we needed to ensure it could quickly and simply transition into a thriving new neighbourhood once the Games have finished.

The project provides a perfect illustration of both the city's broadened horizons and its capacity to deliver. In less than 12 months, we secured a site, issued compulsory purchase orders, started demolition, obtained planning permission and appointed a contractor. We have also approved a funding package of £340m, including £165m from central government.

Most importantly, the team have ensured that the legacy of the Games will be a new high quality residential neighbourhood in the North West of Birmingham at Perry Barr. When competitors depart, the properties will be converted into around 1,400 new homes across a range of affordable and open market tenures.

Achieving this outcome in such a short space of time simply would not have been possible without the vision and culture of collaboration that started in 2010. The whole team has aged in the process, but the project perfectly encapsulates everything that we have been working for in Birmingham. The City showed huge ambition to secure such an iconic global event and demonstrated a huge breadth and depth of skills to ensure it will be delivered in the time available.

Most of all, throughout the entire process everyone kept sight of what we ultimately wanted to achieve; the creation of a secure, diverse and prosperous new neighbourhood that would allow the next generation of local residents to thrive.

Birmingham in the future

In 2019, the transformation of Birmingham city centre is clear to see. Birmingham has seen strong growth in its economy, boosted by transformational development plans, major infrastructure investment, thriving businesses, and successful industry sectors. These factors make Birmingham a location for growing economic success.

The City has a clear trajectory that will shape its future for decades to come. As well as organising the Commonwealth Games, we are also preparing for the arrival of High Speed Two and driving forward a major urban extension, having released 340 hectares of green belt land to accommodate 6,000 homes and a major employment site. East Birmingham, Greater Icknield, and the Ladywood Estate amongst other key growth areas will also see transformational change in the forthcoming years. Across the city, the delivery of significant levels of new housing, jobs and major transport infrastructure will have to keep pace with the needs of the growing population.

I have always believed that we're all capable of so much more than we realise. I have given a lot to Birmingham, but Birmingham has given me – a boy from Birmingham's eastern neighbourhood – so much more.

As we plan the next chapter for this city, the desire to ensure it provides the opportunities for future generations as it provided me, remains the greatest motivation of all.

FOUR PILLARS TO EFFECTIVE DELIVERY

SIR HOWARD BERNSTEIN

SIR HOWARD BERNSTEIN

Sir Howard's career saw a remarkable rise through a local authority, having joined Manchester City Council as Junior Clerk in 1971, and serving for 46 years, with his tenure being characterised by colleagues for his energetic leadership and passion for the city.

He was the Chief Executive of the City Council for 19 years and Head of Paid Service for the Greater Manchester Combined Authority from 2011 – 2017.

Sir Howard was a driving figure in the development of new governance arrangements for the Greater Manchester city-region. He oversaw the establishment of the Greater Manchester Combined Authority (GMCA) in 2011 and the development of the Northern Powerhouse initiative and a series of historical devolution agreements.

From 1996-1999, Sir Howard served as the Chief Executive of Manchester Millennium Ltd which oversaw the transformation of the city centre in the aftermath of the 1996 IRA bombing. He was also instrumental in securing Manchester's hosting of the 2002 Commonwealth Games – then the largest multi-sports event ever hosted in the UK – and the catalyst for the regeneration of East Manchester and the unparalleled investment in sport and leisure facilities focused around the Etihad Campus.

As clerk to Transport for Greater Manchester Committee, and its predecessor bodies, Sir Howard played a leading role in the introduction and expansion of the Metrolink tram network. He was also involved in the establishment of Manchester Airport as a plc in the mid-1980s and the group's ongoing development.

Throughout his career he championed partnerships with government, the private sector and local communities, facilitating a series of transformative projects such as Spinningfields, Manchester Life, NOMA, First Street and the Corridor Manchester innovation district.

Following his retirement from the Council in 2017, Sir Howard was appointed as an Honorary Professor of Politics at the University of Manchester and a strategic advisor to the University on government interactions, healthcare delivery, devolution, culture and international links.

Sir Howard also serves as a strategic advisor to Deloitte, specialising in health and social care, government reform and devolution, and regeneration.

E volving economies, climate pressures, new trade routes and the disruption of traditional industries by technology and innovation are collectively redefining the competitive landscape and growth opportunities for nearly every city in the world.

While growth is a key driver today, it is also not acceptable to deliver economic growth alone. For places to thrive, it is essential there is a core focus on the social aspects of growth, and ensuring residents aren't left behind as a place evolves – in other words, it is a failure of the system if everyone can't participate and share the benefits of progress.

Globalisation has intensified these trends but so have reductions in welfare spending and curtailing public sector wages.

A resulting impact of meeting the challenges created by globalisation and inequality within society is a much higher requirement for infrastructure investment, which in the UK has been underprioritised for too long and is becoming a barrier to the nation's global competitive position as well as domestic mobility and economic connectivity.

Worldwide, communities are demanding more significant influence over the way in which the state discharges responsibilities. This is a healthy and welcomed trend. However, it inevitably manifests in greater fragmentation and polarisation of views, resulting in a need for widespread and sophisticated civic engagement.

Today, younger people are increasingly challenging the conventional approaches to funding services such as social care; older adults are naturally worried about how new funding options will impact on their legacy to their children. Never before has there been a higher duty for local authorities to plot an inclusive and sustainable path for cities.

I am a passionate believer in the transformative power of cities and their central role in creating competitive and resilient national economies. For cities to succeed and sustain themselves they must find their way in a global marketplace, which has become increasingly dynamic and complex, while at the same time meeting the needs of their residents. This requires clear leadership and a focused belief in driving transformation over a sustained time period.

Manchester's post-industrial transition is an example to many towns and cities that a new course can be mapped. Cities can redefine themselves and deliver an urban, social and economic renaissance. Having joined Manchester City Council as a junior clerk in 1971, I spent 46 years serving the city including 19 years as the Chief Executive. In this role, I had a unique opportunity to drive an agenda that reshaped Manchester through innovative new partnerships, economic strategies and governance.

The challenges that faced Manchester are not necessarily unique and will resonate with many other places across the UK and beyond. What was important, above all else, was how we responded to those challenges. In identifying the right path for every town, city or county, the leadership should be asking 'how do we chart a course that benefits all in a dynamic and uncertain world?'

The approach that we took in Manchester can be structured through four key pillars, which can be viewed as the essential components of effective regeneration; growing and diversifying the economic base; civic intervention to ensure people get the support they need to fulfil their potential within growth plans; establishing new ways of generating resources as an enabler of infrastructure investment; and placemaking to ensure the environment is attractive for people to live, work and visit.

Pillar One – planning for growth

Long-term planning and delivery oversight are fundamental.

It is more important than ever to have local authority interventions to support planning and growth. Places must take responsibility for intelligently assessing unique strengths and assets, and how they can be built upon to create new connections and enhance economic ecosystems.

Whether this is new economic clusters, integration into global supply-chains or creating incubators for new industries, all of this needs to be assessed against a backdrop of shifting global trade patterns and technology disruption.

Nationally inspired industrial and economic strategies will always have a role, however, for a place to know whether these strategies are relevant and in its best interests, it should have a clear view of local strengths and unrealised potential to challenge and adapt national frameworks to local priorities.

It is essential to engage residents in meaningful ways to seek their input on local decisions and to help equip them to take greater responsibility for their own social and economic outcomes. Meaningful civic engagement is critical for the legitimacy of local authorities and projects but also the long-term sustainability of plans and investments that depend on residents taking advantage of new opportunities in their city.

Looking at Manchester, the city was one of the biggest manufacturing and production centres in Europe, but post-war globalisation left it with almost nothing but industrial dereliction. However, today's Manchester proves that a successful pivot is possible, with Greater Manchester now one of the UK's biggest commercial and professional centres, a centre for innovation and research with notable scientific achievements, a cultural and creative centre.

Three examples that illustrate the impact of long-term planning in Manchester are the regeneration of Hulme from post-industrial slums and infamous 60's housing experiments to a thriving community; the complete transformation of the city centre in the aftermath of the 1996 IRA bombing; and most recently the emergence of East Manchester as a world-leading sports destination and thriving residential communities in an area that was once the manifestation of Manchester's industrial decline.

The uniting theme across all three examples are a strategic approach linking evidenced growth priorities to spatial and development frameworks that support sustainable change, and give confidence to residents, the surrounding communities and investors that their requirements are understood and recognised.

THE ETIHAD CAMPUS, EAST MANCHESTER. HOME OF MANCHESTER CITY FOOTBALL CLUB

Manchester originated the concept of Strategic Regeneration Frameworks which have now become best practice nationwide and beyond. Fundamentally they encourage public engagement, collaboration with the private sector and other public service providers to set a path that works for all while ensuring the flexibility to respond to changing market dynamics and economic cycles.

Pillar Two – putting people at the core

The UK has a skills deficit in every labour market, with technology and globalisation changing the labour market at pace. Demand also continues to rise for high dependency services such as health, social care, and welfare.

These challenges are compounded by limited national direction on how to reduce demand, a fragmented education system, and housing programmes which are not delivering the homes which are needed.

It is therefore mission critical to help the population build personal capacity and responsibility and provide them with the education and skills they need for today's economic environment.

One powerful source of human opportunity and new career pathways is developing innovation and R&D based economic clusters. These clusters become a platform for attracting talent and new businesses, they enable links and partnerships with the education system and attract further investment as economic enablers due to the pull of supporting companies. Importantly, innovation and R&D based businesses help create a sense of identity and pride.

Innovation in our academic institutions is paramount if we are to maintain a position as an international leader. The landmark merger establishing the University of Manchester was a key strand of our approach. It has helped to reinforce the role of Manchester as a home for science, research and innovation, and boost the competitiveness of Greater Manchester in promising fields such as advanced materials, life sciences, informatics and translational medicine.

Nationwide there is a need for services to help people enter and progress through work rather than services which reinforce the reliance of people on the State. This needs to be highly localised, and delivered efficiently by technology, as new economic pathways emerge.

From a support provision perspective, an essential goal of health and social care policies must be to reduce the demand for high dependency services by preventing individuals from needing these services in the first place, and when that fails, intervening quickly and effectively to help people get back on their feet and move on.

Part of the solution is more place-based models which will see more integrated commissioning, along with new early help and intervention models so that demand for expensive reactive public services can be lessened.

In this regard, the nation needs to see a more significant commitment to devolution for all places which have the ambition, the plans, the maturity of their collaborative structures with business and the capacity to deliver.

Devolution presents the opportunity to re-think the constitutional relationship between local and central government, and is long overdue given the challenges our nation faces for current and future generations.

Right now, we have the most centralised system of government in the Western Hemisphere and a public service offer which has been in need of reform for years.

In Greater Manchester's case the devolution of health services for example was pursued because of the need to exercise more control over the system to change the incentives, to support new models of care in communities, and to create new early help and intervention models to support a transformation in the health of the region's population.

However, Devolution can only work if authorities encourage and facilitate stakeholders joining up their assets and skills, and by creating the platforms for business and academia to participate.

In order to achieve this step change in devolution a clear demonstration of its benefits with sound structure is needed. In the case of Manchester a key priority for us was driving new governance arrangements for the Greater Manchester city-region, the first Combined Authority in the UK outside of London, including the election of a Mayor for Greater Manchester. Aligned to this was the development of the Northern Powerhouse initiative. We followed this with the development of a comprehensive Spatial Plan designed to help shape decisions impacting housing, commercial activity and transport.

Putting the work in upfront resulted in the delivery of four ground breaking devolution agreements with the UK Government that have transferred significant responsibilities for transport, planning and housing, skills, and health and social care services from central government to local authorities in Greater Manchester. These agreements gave local leaders more scope to shape the economic success of the region and reform public services to better address Greater Manchester's needs and priorities.

Pillar Three – creating an environment for fiscal intervention

Towns, cities, and countries need to re-examine approaches to funding infrastructure. Investment needs to be linked to growth objectives, and local places need to be incentivised to grow their economies – which means empowering local authorities to work with businesses to develop their investment models based on local requirements.

These innovative financial instruments to support local investment in infrastructure are exemplified by initiatives such as the Greater Manchester Transport Fund (which has funded Metrolink expansion), the Greater Manchester Housing Investment Fund (which has helped to deliver over 8,000 new homes in Greater Manchester) and the North West Evergreen Fund (which has backed a series of commercially viable and economically significant real estate projects in the North West of England).

Manchester developed individual investment models to support transport, housing, life sciences, the creative industries as well as conventional office and commercial developments. These successful investments have driven significant increases in business rates, upwards of £60m pa and rising, however, local authorities need to be allowed to retain a high proportion of this growth to underpin further investment capability.

This approach requires boldness and ambition - and new skills within the public sector. Manchester invested heavily in a specialist investment team including secondments from the private sector, which now manages a portfolio of nearly £1bn of local assets.

Another critical tool is the ability to secure regional development funding and establish investment structures such as the Greater Manchester Housing and Investment Funds. Undoubtedly these funds helped Greater Manchester mitigate the worst of the 2007 financial crisis.

Through these funds and other instruments over £100m has been invested into over 90 businesses in Greater Manchester creating or safeguarding over 7,150 jobs. Commercial property funds have supported the development of 330,794 sq metres of commercial floor space and the redevelopment of 23 hectares of brownfield land.

To develop and carefully manage these structures, Manchester had to build an internal investment, asset and risk management capability. Today, the resulting impact is multiple investment programmes that are driving change at a pace that would otherwise not have been possible.

UK Government also needs to prioritise more investment in infrastructure - as other countries have been doing for years. For the UK to become competitive with the rest of the world there needs to be much greater transport investment. There also needs to be radical thinking about the pattern of national road and fuel taxation, and how this should be re-thought to support places to reduce congestion and create a new resource for smarter and seamless travel with an emphasis on public transport.

We recognised early on the need to invest in and expand a high-quality public transport network. It has played a key part in productivity gains alongside attracting investment. As the clerk to Transport for Greater Manchester Committee, and its predecessor bodies, there was the opportunity to drive forward the introduction and expansion of the Metrolink tram network. Significantly expanded, the local transport infrastructure, including the Metrolink, has underpinned a sustained increase in social, commercial and economic activity throughout the City since its opening in 1992.

International connectivity is just as vital. Establishing Manchester Airport as a plc in the mid-1980s and the group's ongoing development as a successful commercial operation has helped open up new markets for Greater Manchester and enabled it to compete more effectively worldwide.

Local authorities also have to be pragmatic about working with central government on regeneration efforts regardless of which party is in power. The private sector needs to be engaged early in the strategic planning process and be incentivised to invest through long-term strategic goals that provide certainty, and the potential to achieve fair returns.

As an example, Academic-Private partnerships can facilitate new connections between educational institutions and the private sector to bridge the gap between the classroom/lab and the economy.

Linking up with neighbouring cities builds critical mass and stimulates regional economic development, such as the Greater Manchester Combined Authority or the Northern Powerhouse.

Pillar Four – bringing it all together to create great places to live, work and visit

Positive change can only be achieved through developing an achievable vision that delivers relevant and sustainable growth. Any credible vision must place equal emphasis on the human, economic and physical environment.

A credible vision also requires a great deal of honesty and critical assessment of what's already in place. All too often, local authorities are blind to shifting global dynamics or believe that the 'jobs of yesterday' could return, which regrettably means a credible and pragmatic vision will forever be struggling to get off the ground.

SUNSET OVER DEANSGATE, MANCHESTER

MANCHESTER LIFE'S COTTON FIELD WHARF IN ANCOATS, MANCHESTER

Once an assessment has taken place, the starting point is to build a coherent, ambitious and achievable vision that delivers on policy priorities and gives investors clarity and confidence that investment in the place is truly viable. In this regard, size matters. Plans need to be of sufficient scale and ambition to attract investors, generate meaningful social and economic impact, and have a good chance of attracting funding from central government and capital markets and investors.

Throughout my time at Manchester I have seen the value in championing partnerships with government, the private sector and local communities, facilitating investment into a series of transformative projects such as Spinningfields, NOMA, First Street and the Corridor Manchester innovation district.

Taking a long term partnership approach is vital to securing major investment from institutions and international investors. During my time at Manchester this approach enabled us to attract investment from the Abu Dhabi United Group (owner of the City Football Group, Manchester City FC and Manchester Life Development Company) and a number of Chinese and European institutions, which have delivered significant inward investment and transformed parts of Manchester through a series of major commercial, sports, mixed use, housing, cultural and leisure developments.

It is also critical to be realistic. Every city can benefit from a new art gallery, sports stadium, concert venue or shopping district of a certain size but not every city can sustain an 80,000-capacity stadium or a Louvre-sized museum. It is also vital to take a commercial approach to historic assets; they can be put back to work, but only when it makes cultural and/or business sense to do so.

When it comes to driving progress, local governments need to make things happen, not just stop them from happening. For example, developers who are speculatively land-banking are barriers to growth; they need to be made to build on their land, or hand over to others who will.

Authorities must be prepared to use the tools at their disposal. Successful urban regeneration requires the assertive use of planning instruments by local government, such as strategic regeneration frameworks to set the content and path for neighbourhood development, and compulsory purchase orders to assemble critical land.

Finally, civic leadership must be prepared – in practical and political terms – to step in decisively when external events intervene, or markets fail or experience significant disruption. Regeneration is never a smooth path from vision to completion; it needs leadership, energy and long-term commitment.

BUILDING COMMUNITIES

TONY PIDGLEY CBE

TONY PIDGLEY CBE

Tony is Chairman of the Berkeley Group, a company he founded in 1976 and which now builds more than 3,000 homes a year. He has led some of the country's most challenging and celebrated regeneration programmes, including the reinvention of the Royal Arsenal munitions site in Woolwich and the revival of Hackney's Woodberry Down estate.

At Berkeley, Tony has pioneered a holistic approach to placemaking, which goes beyond the conventional role of a developer. He is passionate about working in partnership with local people to create welcoming communities that inspire civic pride and enhance wellbeing.

Tony has advised successive Governments on regeneration, housing and developing public land. He was a member of Lord Heseltine's Estate Regeneration Advisory Panel, the Thames Estuary 2050 Growth Commission and The Mayor's Outer London Commission. He was the longest serving President in the history of the London Chamber of Commerce and Industry and was awarded a CBE in 2013 for "services to the housing sector and the community".

Tony links his achievements to the lessons and values he learnt in early life. He was adopted by Travellers aged 4, and had an active role in the family business from age 12. He left school at 15 to form his own company in haulage and plant hire. At 19 he sold his business to Crest Homes and became a Building Director, reporting to then Managing Director Jim Farrer. Tony and Jim would later leave Crest to found Berkeley Homes.

The debate around homebuilding can get very technical and cold. It revolves around targets, policies, regulations and planning jargon, which many people don't trust or believe in. Terms like 'affordable housing', 'placemaking' and 'regeneration' are thrown around and often don't mean much. There's a lot of talk and not many people really follow through. So I want to talk about what matters to me.

Good development is all about people. It's about making life better, creating beautiful homes and putting the wellbeing of the whole community at the heart of every plan. It's about creating places people will love as their own and care for long after we've all gone. Good architecture is important but at the end of the day it all comes down to people's quality of life – how they see it, and not us developers or politicians. I've always believed that common sense and decency are free.

But even the best regulations and policies can't make everyone build like this. It has to be something you properly believe in and it comes down to your values. If you respect people, you will listen to them. If you're decent you will make plans to improve their lives. If you have integrity, you will do the right thing over and over again, and you will earn people's trust. None of this is complicated but it amazes me that time and time again this just doesn't happen.

Partnership and collaboration

Good placemaking is always about trust and collaboration. It's just not possible without strong council leadership and a commitment to really engage with local people. Now that doesn't mean we have to agree on every detail. There have been plenty of disagreements over the years! These huge regeneration projects are very demanding. It can last many decades, so there are bound to be problems – politics, the economy and all of the other things life throws up. But when you have a trusting partnership to fall back on, you can always get through. It's about mucking in and getting the job done.

Building a partnership like this is never simple and it's always different from one place to the next. It has to start with a good long look at the local community and lots of conversations. You have to go out of your way to find and listen to people. Then you have to take a blank sheet of paper and start to shape a shared vision that gets to the heart of it and delivers the changes people care about.

But not everyone works like this. Some sites just use fixed ideas and standard designs to save some money. There will be consultations of course, but the process is mostly just for show. In the end, places built like this lack the warmth and welcome of a real community.

When I look at a Berkeley development, I want to see local influence at every level. I want to know who we are talking to and what they told us. I want to see that passion for making life better and going the extra mile to make people happy. At Woodberry Down, for example, our team does small jobs on old parts of the estate we're not building on yet. They don't just care about the current phase – they care about the whole community.

Values and respect

Berkeley has changed a lot over 40 years. But I like to think you can trace some of its core values and culture back to my family's business. My dad Bill traded the old fashioned way and we all mucked in. Horse trading, chopping and selling logs, gardening jobs and groundworks. It wasn't sophisticated but it was entrepreneurial and we always had an eye on the next deal!

I remember we would get paid to clear horse muck from local stables, then sell it on to the fruit nurseries and garden centres. Anyone could have done that, but my dad knew how to talk to people and made sure the stable owners came to us. He listened to them, and they trusted him. That taught me very young that business is all about people.

Courtesy and respect were expected in my house. We were taught that manners are free, and you always say please and thank you. Those rules applied at home, and when we were out dealing with our customers. To a small business like ours, reputation was everything, so there were no shortcuts and we worked long and hard to make people happy. If a customer stopped using us, we would always find out why and learn the lesson.

Another important lesson I learned at home was the value of autonomy. My parents had strict rules but they treated us like adults in many ways and gave us real responsibilities. One of my regular chores was draining the engines on cold nights to stop them freezing, then getting up early to top them back up. That wasn't much fun but it was my task and I took it seriously. After a while I was allowed to drive the lorry and so got even more respect. It doesn't half give a 14-year-old confidence when he gets to drive a massive lorry! Different times back then, of course.

My parents also had us making deals and trades from a very young age, and I bought my first horse aged 12. I loved doing the deal and the more we traded the more excited we got about the next big opportunity. I learned a lot from those early deals, including the importance of cash and speed. If you had the money up front and quick instincts, you could do good business. If you needed credit or a week to think about it, you lost out.

Every Sunday we all counted the money together as a family. This was a serious event and every trade went into my dad's Black Book. His system was very simple. If we'd sold a horse, he would write the price we paid for it in Column A, the best offer we'd had would go in Column B, and the final sale price went in Column C. If we'd sold for less than the highest value my dad would say "that horse owes the family". It was down to the seller to make that up and, make no mistake, you didn't let the family down.

This was my parent's way of giving us a real stake in the business and we all wanted to score high at those book keeping sessions. If we did well, we all ate well. If we did badly, the meat came off the table and we had something to prove the following week. It brought the best out of us, and it's what all Berkeley management teams still do today.

At 15 I left home and left school. I won't share all the details, but it wasn't planned and there was no going back. I had to eat and so I got two paid jobs – one at Tony Saw's Greengrocers in Molesley and the other as a bicycle delivery boy for Mac Fisheries a few streets away on Hampton Court Parade. The rest of the time I worked for myself doing odd jobs like laying turf. I couldn't afford a car so I used that delivery bike to work on my other jobs at night. I will never forget the day when it just couldn't handle any more turf in the basket and it fell to pieces. That day I lost a bicycle and a job!

Before long I saved enough money to buy my own lorry and I can still remember the number plate (SNO 216, in case anyone's interested!), which tells you just how proud I was of it! Now I had the freedom to work for myself full time doing small haulage and groundworks jobs. I'd taken my parents' values to heart and I looked after my customers well.

Gradually I took on more machines and more drivers. And as the company grew, I made sure everyone who worked for me understood what was expected. If I felt I could trust them to do things with care and respect, then I let them run their own rigs and crews. At the end of each week I would give a little bonus to those who had worked the hardest and this worked to motivate everyone! It wasn't a perfect business but I learned a lot and we were the most reliable service in the market and we couldn't grow fast enough.

By the time I was 19 Crest Homes was a big customer. I worked hard to impress Jim Ferrer, one of their directors. I rented a small office in their Walton-on-Thames headquarters, and their Managing Director, Brian Skinner, would drop in and teach me how to do my first proper cash book. Eventually Jim and Brian decided to make an offer for my business, with me joining the main Crest board as part of the deal. I made a few quid off this deal but quickly came down to earth when they took my lorries off me and put me in charge of construction. At 19 I had never built a house, and was now responsible for delivering hundreds of homes and dozens of sites. But Brian and Jim didn't need technical expertise, they wanted to change the culture, so that's what I did at Crest.

A few years later Brian stepped down as MD through ill-health and not long after that, Jim and I left Crest to form Berkeley together. From day one we put those values into everything we did. Right into the DNA. Respect, customer focus and a passion for getting every last detail just right; those have been the Berkeley hallmarks from day one. The business has gone from building around a dozen homes a year to creating whole new neighbourhoods. But our culture and values are the same. That will never change and that's what makes the difference.

Woodberry Down, Hackney

What frustrates me most about the placemaking debate is that people talk too much about physical changes and not enough on the social side. I always approach it the other way round. People come first, everything else follows. Our partnership at Woodberry Down shows why this matters.

Ten years ago we started to work with Woodberry Down Community Organisation, Hackney Council and Genesis Housing to transform this run down estate. There was already a masterplan in place and a consultation process had run its course. But Berkeley was new to the estate, the people didn't know us, and they were worried what might happen. So we started by getting to know them.

We walked the streets, held meetings, open days and exhibitions. We visited people's homes and had more cups of tea than I could count. We built mock-up flats people could walk around, see for themselves and make suggestions on how to make them better. Hundreds of residents came along and it made a real difference. They could see we were listening and we started to earn their trust.

We quickly learned how passionately people felt about the reservoirs next to the estate, so we restored the banks and created a bridge link and boardwalk so everyone could enjoy the water's edge for the first time in decades. Later we changed the masterplan so the reservoirs became the centrepiece of the new Woodberry Down. This led to our partnership with the London Wildlife Trust and the creation of the Woodberry Wetlands, a beautiful 27 acre nature reserve, open to everyone all year round.

These ideas didn't come from an architect's studio. They took shape gradually, through hundreds of conversations with hundreds of different people. They came from the ground up and that's why local people love them.

It was such a success that we established a Residents' Design Committee. This gives advice on everything from masterplan principles to where you plug in your kettle and make a cuppa. We provided architectural training and funded a design adviser to help people learn about the industry and make informed choices. At the end of the day, we just treated people with respect. The committee's feedback shaped many features of the development and we went on to build many affordable homes with separate kitchens rather than open plan. We listened to what the residents told us they wanted. There's still more to do but people are on side and the community is getting stronger. But we never take that for granted.

Royal Arsenal, Woolwich

The Royal Arsenal site in Woolwich was a completely different kind of challenge. When I first went there in the 1990s it was derelict, cut-off and contaminated. There were no people and it was a complete wasteland. Across the road, Woolwich town centre was suffering high unemployment and all of the social problems that come with it. I remember walking around the area and thinking that this would take a lot of vision to transform.

Twenty years later, Royal Arsenal has become a beautiful riverside neighbourhood and has helped Woolwich get back on its feet. I am really proud of what has happened here. It is now a safe and welcoming home, with jobs and opportunities for local people. Again, it all comes back to partnership. This time with the Royal Borough of Greenwich, the GLA, and the local community. We have faced hundreds of challenges along the way but we've all mucked in together to get this fantastic new place built.

We started by restoring the heritage buildings and opening up the site with new public spaces. We brought down the security fences, created the first new homes, and re-connected the site with the community around it. People started to come in and have a look around. We worked hard to give them the facilities they had asked for. Gradually we opened up pubs, cafés, shops, offices, a medical centre, pharmacy, the Academy of Performing Arts, a brewery, and a crèche.

Working closely with the council, we managed to persuade Marks & Spencer to open here, something no one thought was possible in the early days. We helped two local people grow their catering business from their kitchen, to a market stall and then into a beautiful restaurant. We helped another local creative start-up grow to take over a 140 sq.m. office.

Our partnership really showed its strength when the Crossrail route was being finalised. The Royal Arsenal station was not part of the plan and Woolwich was about to miss an incredible opportunity. So Chris Roberts, then Greenwich Council Leader, asked me to go with him to the Department for Transport to change their minds. We made our case, with Berkeley committing £23m to the programme and taking responsibility for building the station box. We got it. Woolwich would be connected to the rest of London, and beyond.

We worked with the South East London Chamber of Commerce to run business forums and networking events that create links between Woolwich traders. We also took the decision to base our own permanent divisional office at Royal Arsenal. This means we're a developer, investor, commercial tenant, and major local employer. We know the local community inside-out, we talk to everyone, and we know what really matters to local people.

Those who remember the old Woolwich of the 1990s will understand how far it has come. Many factors contributed to this success but at the heart of it all is a partnership based on trust and a shared vision. The case study is summarised on page 54.

RESTORED BUILDINGS AND PUBLIC REALM AT ROYAL ARSENAL

Royal Arsenal Riverside – case study

SIZE AND SCALE	5,100 homes, 53,800 sq.m. commercial space across 35 hectare site.
USES	Royal Arsenal is a safe and welcoming home, a thriving cultural scene, and a vital source of employment. Facilities include a hotel, shops, restaurants, offices, gyms, a nursery and health centre. A new 16,000 sq.m. creative district including performance spaces and a theatre. 25% of the 5,100 homes will be affordable.
INFRASTRUCTURE	A new onsite Crossrail station box and Thames Clipper passenger pier; over 3 hectares of new high quality public realm and a new 1.6 hectare public park.
PARTNERS	Partnership between Berkeley Homes, the Royal Borough of Greenwich and Greater London Authority. Onsite affordable housing providers include Southern Housing, Optivo, Moat and Notting Hill Housing.
TIMESCALES	30 year development scheme set to complete in 2029.
IMPACTS	100 onsite businesses with over 2,200 jobs, 1000's of additional visitors and a community of more than 10,000 people and wider community benefits including a re-energised Woolwich Town Centre.
LOCATION	On the southern bank of the Thames in Woolwich, London, with 1 km of river frontage. Connected to central London via the new Crossrail station, Woolwich Railway station and Thames Riverbus services. The site is in close proximity to Woolwich Town Centre.
HISTORY OF THE SITE	Munitions manufacturing site which at the peak of its use during World War I employed 80,000 people. Role declined throughout the course of the 20th Century with the facility closing in 1994. The site contains 23 listed buildings.
THE STRATEGY	Masterplan produced to create a whole new neighbourhood where the site's heritage, including all 23 listed buildings, is integrated with modern buildings and spaces to create a successful place.
CHALLENGES TO DELIVERY	The closure of the site in 1994 had a negative impact on the wider area leading to economic decline, low values and a degraded environment. The site itself was severely contaminated by decades of munitions production and the 23 listed buildings were in a derelict state.
PROCUREMENT PROCESS	The Freeholder London Development Agency (LDA) and Berkeley Homes entered into a Development Agreement in 2001. Acquisition of the listed buildings enabled a larger scale masterplan. In 2011 Berkeley Homes acquired the LDA freehold to unlock the delivery of the Crossrail station, with further land acquired from the Royal Borough of Greenwich to expand the masterplan further.

ROYAL ARSENAL, WOOLWICH BEFORE ITS REGENERATION

ROYAL ARSENAL, WOOLWICH TODAY AS A MAJOR MIXED USE DEVELOPMENT

Infrastructure and transformation

When you look at places which have really transformed and grown over the last 30 years or so, it often starts with new infrastructure. It's not always the most glamorous or profitable part of the process, but laying these critical foundations is essential. In London the success of Canary Wharf, King's Cross, Stratford, Woolwich and Nine Elms are all driven by major investment in transport, and the other amenities and spaces that make these places work.

The same is true outside London. High Speed 2 is a key driver for the incredible transformation happening right now across Birmingham, and towns like Slough and Reading are making great progress thanks to the imminent arrival of Crossrail 1. It will be many years before we really appreciate the enormous benefits these bold transport projects are bringing to the people and communities all along their routes.

At a human level, these major infrastructure projects help to give more people a good home and new opportunities in their day to day lives. At a strategic level, they create the right conditions for enduring growth and regeneration. They breed confidence and encourage all the partners involved to raise their aspirations and think about how a place could really improve and change for the better.

Over the years Berkeley has contributed to many strategic infrastructure projects including new Tube links, bypasses, bridges and even piers. In every case I ask myself two simple questions:

1   Will this make life better for the local community?

2   Will it enable new growth and homes?

If the answers to both is a clear 'yes', then it's a sound long term investment. Take our Kidbrooke Village development in Greenwich for example. As the community grew we worked with the council and the rail authorities to increase capacity at Kidbrooke Station through a temporary expansion scheme. Next, we will deliver a permanent overhaul that will integrate a bright new station within a buzzing new village centre. By embedding new infrastructure within a mix of new amenities, shops and public space we can really drive change and create a much better place for the whole community.

Despite all these success stories, I worry that infrastructure is still not the top investment priority it should be. We have certainly moved in the right direction in recent years, but the housing crisis demands a bolder approach and I'd like to see more spending power passed down to devolved authorities and local councils. That's where you find the passion, vision and local knowledge you need to make things happen.

A long-term approach

If you think back to the early 1990s, there was very little regeneration going on across London. There were many unused industrial sites going to ruin but very few developers wanted to take them on. As the housing market recovered, we could see the great potential of these sites and Berkeley started to explore how we could bring them back into use. A major stumbling block was funding. Brownfield urban regeneration costs a huge amount up front and takes years to generate a return. We knew borrowing would be far too expensive and risky, so we raised equity from our shareholders.

This decision goes back to my values of autonomy and ability to move quickly in the market. It gave us the balance sheet strength to take on long-term regeneration programmes and to keep our independence. We didn't need to consult the banks over every investment decision. We could employ capital over a much longer time frame than you could with a traditional lender. We had greater freedom and autonomy than a geared developer and we could use our reserves to move quickly in the market. We had the advantage of 'cash and speed', just like my family's horse trading business.

Major brownfield regeneration was new territory for Berkeley, and we had to learn quickly. We were now remediating badly contaminated sites that had lain in a shocking state for decades. We embraced partnerships, working closely with councils, mayors, community groups and local people to tackle a whole range of issues. We focused on the long term revival of our sites and the communities around them. We started to think about how to create places with real warmth and character. Places that inspire a sense of pride and belonging, with the right mix of beautiful public spaces, natural landscapes and valuable amenities that bring people together to enjoy community life.

But throughout this our company culture and values stayed the same. As we grew, we made sure our management teams had the autonomy that drives innovation and creative thinking. This agile, long-term approach is still at the heart of Berkeley Group's business model. This explains why we are one of the few developers able to invest in London during today's volatile market conditions.

Kidbrooke Village, North Greenwich

If you are going to transform an area and build a community that long-term approach is essential. One of the most compelling examples of this is Kidbrooke Village in North Greenwich where we have taken a notorious Council Estate and transformed it.

By the end of the 1990s, the Ferrier Estate community was beset by crime, unemployment and entrenched social problems. Royal Mail refused to deliver here and with a Ferrier postcode on your CV it was harder to find work. The estate was dark, enclosed and in severe disrepair.

Today, it is a thriving community, with more than 1,600 new homes built so far, a village centre, a skills training centre and 86 acres of stunning parks and wetlands. People of all ages and backgrounds enjoy fêtes, festivals, clubs, markets, volunteering days and old fashioned get-togethers.

But to achieve all this, the first crucial task was to earn the community's trust. Many Ferrier residents didn't believe the estate could become an open landscape with amenities and shops. They didn't know our team and they didn't believe we would build good quality homes for their families and neighbours.

So we met them face to face, and listened to their concerns. They told us they wanted pitched roofs on their new homes, so we changed the design. They felt a proposed ball court was too close to their homes, so we moved it.

While building the first phase, we invited them in to inspect our work and we went beyond the specification, improving finishes, adding outdoor taps and designing bespoke storage spaces for bins, pushchairs and bikes. Local people could see the care and attention going into their homes and we earned their respect.

When the credit crunch hit there was a fresh crisis of confidence and residents feared the work would stop. It caused real anxiety and distress. So, with the support of the community and council, we accelerated the affordable home building programme, rehoused Ferrier residents ahead of schedule and demolished what was left of the old estate.

We brought forward investment in vital social infrastructure, building a temporary village centre with a Sainsbury's, doctors' surgery, dentist, café and local store. And we put our heart and soul into the landscape, creating a beautiful natural setting for everyone to enjoy. The contrast with the old Ferrier Estate could not have been clearer and the local community embraced the change.

All this has had a huge impact on many residents' lives. One local mum told us that her boys started crying with excitement when they saw their own garden, and that they started to sleep through the night for the first time. The eldest boy went on to train with us and has his own home in the village. His mum is a member of the Residents' Association.

Our core team, who are based in the village, are well known to the community and many have been there from the start. They are involved in everyday life; solving problems and looking for ways to make things better. They recently installed a swan crossing on Tudway Road after residents reported a near miss.

Some exceptional public spaces, homes and amenities have been created at Kidbrooke Village, but that doesn't explain why this community has thrived. The real lesson is that we need to focus on people, not plans, and approach every small decision with their wellbeing in mind. The case study is summarised on page 60.

FERRIER ESTATE KIDBROOKE, LONDON

Kidbrooke Village – case study

SIZE AND SCALE	£1bn investment, 4,966 homes, 8,361 sq.m. of commercial space, 35 hectares of parkland across a 109 hectare site.
USES	A mixed and sustainable community, with a mix of homes, shops, schools, squares, parks, and wetlands. The site includes 35% affordable housing, a new village centre, mix of commercial space and community and health facilities.
INFRASTRUCTURE	£143m committed to infrastructure including 5,203 sq.m. community space, train station building and a primary school.
PARTNERS	Partnership between the Royal Borough of Greenwich, the Greater London Authority, Berkeley Homes and three Registered Social Landlords – Southern Housing Group, Optivo and Moat. The London Wildlife Trust is a partner managing the parks in collaboration with local residents.
TIMESCALES	Commenced in 2009 the 30 year development scheme has already delivered 1,800 homes of which 43% are affordable.
IMPACTS	Rejuvenated community providing high quality of life for existing and new residents, dedicated construction skills training centre, 140 apprenticeships, 205 permanent jobs, and 1000's of construction jobs.
LOCATION	Located in the Royal Borough of Greenwich, south east London. Central London is 20 minutes by train from the nearby Kidbrooke Station.
HISTORY OF THE SITE	The Ferrier Estate was built between 1968 and 1972. By the 1980s it had become one of the most economically deprived areas in the country.
THE STRATEGY	Identified as one of the most ambitious regeneration schemes in Europe. Benefiting from a collaborative public-private delivery model early investment in social housing, creating a temporary village centre and community amenities has been key to the success establishing community buy-in and providing a focal point for residents.
CHALLENGES TO DELIVERY	Bad design and an enclosed inward-looking layout created an isolated site with entrenched social problems that required a comprehensive approach to addressing. Early interventions required to deliver infrastructure providing focal point for the newly emerging community. Important delivery of social housing in first two phases created significant cashflow challenge.
PROCUREMENT PROCESS	OJEU compliant tender process with a partnership Development Agreement signed in 2007.

THE FERRIER ESTATE BEFORE ITS TRANSFORMATION INTO KIDBROOKE VILLAGE

KIDBROOKE VILLAGE TODAY

Rebuilding trust

All of my experience tells me that great places come when developers, councils and communities embrace partnership, think long-term and work hard to trust each other. If we get this right, we can always create real communities that stand the test of time.

What frustrates me is that our society is less trusting than it used to be. On many levels we've become more bureaucratic, and less collaborative and helpful. What used to be a quick and simple decision between two partners is now an ordeal. Instead of solving problems with a conversation and trying to help each other, we end up going through complex processes that add no value whatsoever. This has made homebuilding much slower and more complicated. Here are three examples:

Firstly, when I bought my first home on Felix Lane in Shepperton I nicked it for £500. I paid half in cash and the rest in an 'I owe you'. No agents, no banks, no solicitors and I got the deeds and the keys in about a week. How have we got so far away from this?

Secondly, my first planning application was to Elmbridge Borough Council. I got an appointment with the planner, Brian Salmon, and we went through the drawings. He told me to move one home back from a neighbour's fence and make the porch a little bigger. Six weeks later I had planning permission.

Finally, when I needed my first bank loan I walked into my local branch and the manager sat down with me to fill out the forms and write up my business plan. He knew I wasn't great with paperwork and he wanted to help me. Today you're treated like a criminal if you ask for a loan and the self-employed can't get a mortgage.

For a young developer now, these stories must seem like a different world. When I was still a teenager running my first business I had to approach the Inland Revenue for the first time. It started off as a cash business run out of the old railway carriage I was living in at the time. It goes without saying that I didn't have much of a bookkeeping system. I knew it couldn't go on, and when I went to the tax office to sort things out I was terrified. They could have thrown the book at me, but instead they helped me.

They were pleased to learn about a successful young businessman and they took me through the system with respect and courtesy. I'm not sure today's tax system would be so supportive. We need to change that culture and get back to being helpful and decent to each other.

Until we really embrace trust and partnership, homebuilding will remain difficult and slow. We have to get this balance right because this housing crisis is causing society real pain. Too many people are losing hope and feel let down by a country that won't reward their hard work with a good home. We have to change this.

We all agree that everyone in society deserves a good home. Everyone has a right to their own front door and a warm, safe place that meets their needs. It doesn't matter if it's private, affordable or rented. A good home fills us with pride and gives us a real stake in society. The challenge is to get everyone involved, from the government, developers, councils, housing associations and communities, and to put people at the heart of homebuilding; working together in the spirit of partnership.

DELIVERING LEGACY
THROUGH PLACE MAKING

HELEN GORDON

HELEN GORDON

Helen is Chief Executive of Grainger plc the UK's largest listed residential landlord.

Since taking on the role of Chief Executive in 2016 Helen has accelerated the company's development of new build to rent communities throughout the UK.

Helen's background has been in mix use development and public and private partnerships, with 40 years of experience. She spent 10 years at John Laing Developments and 6 years at Milton Keynes Development Corporation.

Helen has held senior positions including Global Head of Real Estate Asset Management at RBS, Director of Legal and General Property, with responsibility for the Main Life Fund and circa 8 smaller Funds including the English Cities Fund, and Head of Development and Group Property Director of Railtrack.

Helen sits on the Board of Derwent London as a non-executive Director and is currently a Board Director of the European Public Real Estate Association and President of the British Property Federation. Helen has held a number of non-exec positions and Government appointments including the Board of Covent Garden Market Authority, Board of British Waterways, was a Trustee for The College of Estate Management for nine years and an advisory board member of Cambridge University's Land Economy Department.

Helen is a member of RICS and has a degree in Estate Management from Oxford Polytechnic (now Oxford Brookes).

I frequently say to the team at Grainger that I believe we have the privilege and the responsibility of enhancing people's lives; how people live, interact and socialise. Throughout my career I have been fortunate to have had the opportunity to shape places and influence how people work, shop, relax, and travel. I realised the power of buildings on people's lives from a very young age and the importance of being able to imagine the impact of well planned, designed, and managed environments.

When I was three years old my parents built their own home and I can just about remember the feeling of excitement as each weekend I was taken to site to see the progress. From that moment I was hooked on the building process, that home and the thought my parents put into it shaped how we lived as a family and ensured a happy childhood until I left it for college.

Now, even though my parents moved 25 years later, it still has an impact on how we spend time as a family; it is still influenced by that first home. Our home was also where all the other children congregated. The safe places for play were always enhanced by parents who would organise games and thus this home and our neighbourhood was better for the investment they made in building community in our back garden!

If we can build quality buildings and spaces then we can support healthy and happy people. In my mind the key to achieving this and building sustainable growth and productivity in the built environment is to build in resilience into our developments. Creating these resilient environments requires a focus on three ingredients; plan like you are never going to leave; plan with people at the heart; and study the past to define the future.

It is essential for all long term land owners and for all of those charged with defining our future towns and cities to evaluate schemes against these three key criteria. This approach should also be adopted by trader developers and house builders as a means of ensuring a legacy of valuable and well regarded places. However, successful environments are not just about the buildings, it is also essential to consider how you maintain, manage, and curate them for the future.

The delivery of great places and the dialogue about it has focused on the design of the buildings, spaces and infrastructure but it is equally important to understand the investment that is required in creating opportunities for communities to come together and to enjoy public and private spaces. How we create communities is so often overlooked.

This linkage between health and wellbeing and productivity has been around for centuries. In the early 1800s the philanthropic towns movement began in the UK and in the mid 1850s Titus Salts' development of Saltaire, on the River Aire, was launched and is widely regarded as an example of enlightened 19th Century urban planning.

This was quickly followed by the Lever Brothers at Port Sunlight [work commenced in 1888], the Cadbury family at Bournville in 1893 and many others. These early industrialists recognised something which I believe that as a nation we do not attach sufficient focus to, they recognised that the good quality home environment gives rise to an increase in happiness, health, and importantly productivity.

Titus Salt at Saltaire provided homes, parks, schools, hospitals, community halls, sports facilities, and places of worship. The lives of his workers were dramatically improved. The philanthropists designed and built as if they were never going to leave and 170 years later, and a long time after the wool manufacturing has ceased, Saltaire remains an enjoyable and popular place to live in Yorkshire and a UNESCO World Heritage site. This link between the buildings and villages they created and improving lives was seen as philanthropic compared to their peers at the time but the resultant improvements drove employee loyalty and productivity, and therefore strong commercial returns.

The resilient philanthropists had a long term plan that put people at the heart and were carefully planned with reference to heritage of the environment and the products that they were creating. The first philanthropic developers approach to planning did not come into wider currency until the post war planning acts of the 1940s. Probably the best example was actually outside the planning acts with the new towns movement when once again people had the opportunity to create a longer term vision for a whole area.

Today we rarely have the opportunity, in a single ownership, to develop a town. Early in my career I was fortunate enough to be involved in the development of one of the UK's most well renowned new towns – Milton Keynes.

Whilst I was reading Estate Management we visited a number of areas requiring regeneration and the new towns that were emerging in the late 1970s. In quick succession we visited the derelict London Docklands and Milton Keynes new town. I remember going with colleagues, many of which were dismissive of the uniformity of the design and critical that Milton Keynes was soulless, and arguing that the standard of the housing the residents had versus the standard of the derelict homes we saw in the Docklands of London provided a quality of life that was much better.

Some three years later I was given the opportunity to work in Milton Keynes and found a team of planners, architects and surveyors dedicated to improving lives. The first Chairman, Lord Campbell of Eskan (Jock), was fastidious about the new city, and like hundreds of people that went through more than 25 years of the early years of building the city, he was committed to improving lives as well as providing a practical resilient environment.

Milton Keynes today is a thriving successful city with more than 150 company headquarters and many technology start-up companies. It has a mixture of housing of all tenures and values; it has greenery, parks, walkways, it has the right ratio of schools. The pioneers of Milton Keynes; that worked on the design and development of this new city, needed to secure a hospital and a railway station.

One of the most successful things about Milton Keynes was not only the quality and commitment of the designers working on the city, but also the quality and commitment from those working in community liaison.

The city was defined by a number of grid squares, each one acting as a neighbourhood and each one having a community neighbourhood officer. New residents would be welcomed and introduced to their community and all its facilities, and friendship and support networks were created, the result of which was that the residents of Milton Keynes were the biggest ambassadors for the city.

In a city where people had moved away from their old family links to a completely new area to start a new and better life, the designers of the city recognised that putting people at the heart of the city, which was previously green fields, would require a deep social investment in creating ownership and responsibility for the environment. They also understood that people's health and well-being and their productivity was essential for the new companies that were attracted by a vibrant new labour force. All of this would be influenced by how they had bonded with their new city, their neighbourhood, and their homes.

The Milton Keynes plan, which was a series of neighbourhoods, probably lacked one thing which made its success harder to understand initially, and that was the lack of historic anchors. The planners and designers worked on the plan ensuring the development around the few historic settlements and buildings but the relatively flat and lightly populated rural landscape didn't give us the opportunity to anchor buildings and spaces with historic references at a density we would have liked. During that time I felt it was easier to attract overseas businesses into Milton Keynes than to achieve relocations of UK businesses and it was possibly as we got higher density buildings and civic amenities including things like the leisure districts, theatres and galleries that Milton Keynes dropped its negative persona and reached a critical mass that makes it the success it is today.

It was during my six years working in Milton Keynes and being responsible for the central area office and mixed use development that I realised, almost 20 years before people started talking about the importance of place making, that when you design a building you must think of the neighbourhood, when you design a neighbourhood you must think of the city and when you get that very rare opportunity to work on the development of a city, you need to think about it in its country and global context; it is important to plan for more than 100 years.

Milton Keynes had a very clear long term plan which is at the heart of its resilience. Its design around the growth of car movements and the wide grid road system, which perhaps now looks like an over provision, is central to this. The network of cycle routes (Redways) separated cyclist and pedestrians from cars. The roads are wide enough to take public transport in the future and even the provision of and protection of a route for a further central area tram route are examples of future proofing.

This experience of a combination of master planning, public consultation and financing took me through my career. For 10 years working at John Laing I was engaged in all aspects of property including from the first shopping centre in Belfast to the first regeneration building in the Jewellery Quarter in Birmingham, and from offices to eventually one of the first privately developed railways stations, Ashford International.

That work then took me to head of the development team at the newly privatised Railtrack.

It was here that I realised the breadth of stakeholders that are affected and also it was here that gave me the insight into how people really feel about the building that they regularly use. Virtually everybody I met would talk about 'my' station and whilst we often talk about 'my' home, regardless of whether it is owned or not, it is working on some of these public buildings that I realised the importance of the public feeling. They owned it and the public consultation needed to be much wider than the immediate community.

Such was the degree of engagement with rail user groups, regulators, local community, and commuters that the development team on each and every scheme built a consultation matrix. This ensured that we were regularly talking to people about the plans for 'their' station. This approach led to the speed and success in achieving some of the enhancements that Railtrack had ambitions for.

Established on the experience of a highly successful redevelopment of Liverpool Street station in the late 1980s, Railtrack had a vision for its major stations and the improvements and impacts it can have on the lives of thousands of travellers, particularly commuters. It is sometimes forgotten that rail travel was in decline at the time of privatisation and this was an industry with Victorian infrastructure which has had to cope with a massive increase in passenger numbers.

The three criteria for development of: plan like you are going to be there forever; putting people at the heart of it; and understanding the heritage, were absolutely executed in the major stations and development team's work. I sometimes find it difficult to remember Paddington before the development of the Lawn area at the entrance or Birmingham New Street, London Bridge and Kings Cross before their major interventions. These projects were 20 years in the making and each one of them started with a real deep understanding of the heritage, the way people used and moved through the station and the great affection people had for their station.

Throughout my career I have had fantastic opportunities to work with great architects from Renzo Piano, Foster and Partners, Nick Grimshaw, Wilkinson Eyre and Richard Rogers. It was in the context of these great and important heritage buildings that Railtrack invested in high quality architecture.

During this time I took on my first serious non-executive board appointment. I was appointed to the board of British Waterways (now the Canal & River Trust). The parallels of the estate of the Victorian designed railways and the Victorian designed canal infrastructure in England and Scotland made this a logical appointment. It was a remarkable time for the waterways. There was a thrilling combination of a strong visionary leadership at the centre and in the regions, together with a supportive government, and the new millennium projects and lottery funding. Regeneration, renewal, and new projects were launched in most major cities from Glasgow to Manchester, Birmingham and London.

The team at British Waterways, supported by their joint venture partners, sought to design high quality environments that leveraged the valuable historic waterway environment and its contribution to people's leisure and recreation, enabling access and amenity and in doing so opened up the waterways to a new generation.

Following Railtrack's move back into the public sector I moved to work at Legal & General with the responsibility for the £5bn Life Fund (2003).

The Legal & General Life Fund had been established for many years and its purpose was to use long term property investment to provide above average returns to investors. The age and size of the fund enabled it to take some less conventional investments including a high proportion of development activity. It also had a large strategic land portfolio and co-invested with others in a variety of funds. At the time it dominated the Legal & General property business but was also an enabler to attract investment and create co-investment opportunities.

I had the privilege to lead the team of talented fund, asset and development managers that were engaged in ground breaking projects from major strategic land sites to core parts of the City of London and London's West End. The value and importance of the sites and the reputation of Legal & General meant our approach was meticulous and patient, and mindful of our role of creating wealth, whilst leaving a legacy of high quality schemes.

It was the Life fund that created, with English Partnerships and MUSE, the English Cities Fund. Chaired by Sir Michael Lyons, it funded and delivered regeneration projects in Liverpool, Plymouth, Canning Town (London), and Salford.

One of the schemes I had the privilege to work on in my role at L&G was the new Bloomberg London headquarters. As new philanthropists, the likes of Bloomberg and Google, who in the thought that they give to their buildings are influencing the well-being and productivity of their employees today.

I came to the Bloomberg headquarters project at a very early stage in its development, including the review and selection of an architect. The brief was very clear, it was designed to raise the bar for future office buildings and there was a desire to provide space which energises employees, clients, and visitors by encouraging a new level of productivity. This productivity was seen as being considerably enhanced by the opportunities for people to meet within the building and to engage and exchange information.

Two key features that were fundamental were the concept of the pantry and the helix. Rather than a canteen in a discreet area of the building, the pantry became the hub through which all employees went through to have those occasional conversations and moments of interaction as well as being a source of healthy snacks. There was also the desire to eliminate discreet lifts that went to various floors avoiding interaction by making very open lifts. The triple-helix, which is a ramp within the building, is wide enough to allow people to engage as they move between floors. Every decision made on the construction of the Bloomberg building was made with employees and the surrounding community in mind.

Michael Bloomberg is clearly an inspirational business leader but he also has a very strong commitment to build a better future, from his work in the foundation of Bloomberg and as a former Mayor of New York. Going back to the three key criteria, he had a very clear plan and vision of what he wanted to achieve.

The reason I worked with the Blomberg team is that the fund that I was responsible for at Legal & General owned the site and we were initially trying to lease a newly created building to them. It soon became apparent that the level of investment and the complexity of the design could not work on a traditional rental model and we leased the site alone, thereby allowing the occupier the freedom to experiment and innovate.

Being an owner occupier of the building enabled him to plan for the long term. He built the building with his people in mind and the work that he did in informing the brief around the heritage of the site, including the preservation of the Temple of Mithras, the aspects to St Paul's and St Stephen's Wallbrook, and utilising the roman road Watling Street as a natural thoroughfare for eating and drinking establishments resonate with a piece of the art work by Olafur Eliasson within the building which has the statement 'No Future is Possible Without a Past'. 55% of the space on the ground floor is open and the scheme includes a new Bank tube station entrance.

The Bloomberg website, which includes a tour of the building, references the fact that the building's future success is on the inside and outside and that it honours the past. All three criteria to good development can be found in this scheme. The building was awarded the winner of the Stirling Prize 2018.

The other major scheme that I had the opportunity to work on was the development of Central Saint Giles, a block at the top of end of Covent Garden close to Centre Point and Denmark Street (Tin Pan Alley). Central Saint Giles is a mixed use scheme, it comprises offices, restaurants, private housing and social housing around a beautifully landscaped piazza. On the site there was an ugly building occupied by the government which was thought to house MI6 and be the inspiration for the Circus in Tinker Tailor Soldier Spy.

The redevelopment scheme was designed by Renzo Piano, his first building in London before The Shard. It is, in my opinion, a beautiful environment. My friends and colleagues in architecture and design were excited about its prospects. I love the design, its colourful glazed terracotta façades reflecting Tin Pan Alley, and I cherished the opportunity of working with a leading architect. What for me was the most rewarding was the work we did with the community, not just through the design and planning process.

Our activity on community engagement stepped up after we got planning consent. This was not as a requirement of any planning agreement, it was our clearly stated aim to get our neighbours to appreciate the environment that we were creating. We and our joint venture partner, Mitsubishi Estates, were investing c.£450m. Mitsubishi Estates came with the same approach as ours, of long term planning. Their original business had designed the Marunouchi district in Japan from the early 1900s and they still owned and curated most of the space which is one of the most beautiful parts of Tokyo.

Mitsubishi Estates were a very willing participant in all of the community work, whether it was with the church or the local primary school. This work included helping the children understand the new area that we were creating and how the development process came about, but also we ensured the site workforce and all suppliers were as engaged with the community. Virtually every subcontractor on the site engaged with the school, building places for the parents to wait, designing a stage so that their hall could put on small concerts, redecorating rooms, and helping the school in general. In return we were rewarded with a community that adored our project, understood it, and were great advocates for it.

This area of London is surprisingly residential, albeit at the top of the theatre district, with a strong night time economy. The children we were working with, some as young as six or seven, are the teenagers of the future whom we hope will still remain proud of their involvement and engagement in a new public piazza in their neighbourhood. The philosophy behind the project meant that we wanted a lot of open spaces and permeability. It was the first office building of its type in London to have public space enclosed with work stations where people could sit as an alternative to a coffee shop or a hotel lobby with their laptop or with their book and pause for a moment.

Renzo Piano wanted his vision to be understood and held 'Piano lessons' in the piazza. Our Japanese partners held a concert in the lobby as well as art exhibitions. The quality of the social housing and the private for sale housing and the use of terraces, winter gardens and open space, means that this high density building provides permeability and transparency as well as an environment that occupiers, visitors and residents recognise as a special part of this area of London. Implementing this scheme and chairing the joint venture was one of the most interesting and enjoyable parts of my career. The case study is summarised on page 76.

When I left Legal & General in 2011 the Life Fund was the highest performing fund in its peer group and it had a legacy of amazing projects.

CENTRAL ST GILES

Central St Giles – case study

SIZE AND SCALE	1.75 acres. One of the largest developments in the heart of London's West End.
USES	408,000 sq. ft. of offices, 109 apartments (50% affordable), 25,000 sq. ft. of restaurants and cafes, public piazza, 17,000 sq. ft. roof terraces.
INFRASTRUCTURE	Indoor and outdoor public realm, a new piazza with public art, offsite contributions to local signage, gardens and community uses.
PARTNERS	Mitsubishi Estates, Legal & General, Circle Anglia and United House.
TIMESCALES	Planning permission granted 2006, fully let by 2011.
IMPACTS	A colourful mixed use scheme in the heart of London's West End designed to attract international media companies to remain in this area of London and to create permeability on this previously closed site.
LOCATION	In a dense part of London at a point which links Bloomsbury, Covent Garden, Soho and Fitzrovia. A short distance from Centrepoint.
HISTORY OF THE SITE	Once one of the worst slums in London, known as the Rookery, it housed thousands of destitute people before being redeveloped in the 1950's for government office blocks, which were built around a courtyard with no public access.
THE STRATEGY	The Legal & General Life Fund team worked with Renzo Piano and Stanhope to create a St Giles Renaissance forum as a focal point for residents and community groups to influence the regeneration of the area.
CHALLENGES TO DELIVERY	The site adjoined a conservation area but was also in an area where Ken Livingston (the then Mayor of London) wanted to see tall towers. This put the solution to the site at risk from competing forces. The exemplar design and inclusion of residential together with high quality public realm were used to counterbalance conflicting design demands. Renzo Piano agreed to take on the commission because the company was all about lasting quality.
PROCUREMENT PROCESS	The site was owned historically by Legal & General, with partners selected to help finance and deliver.

CENTRAL ST GILES: OPENING UP INTERNAL AND EXTERNAL MEETING PLACES TO REINTRODUCE VIBRANCY

In my very early days prior to entering into development and master planning I worked for a year in property management. I feel that this is one of the great foundations for anybody who wants to be a developer. It is essential to understand what it means to keep people within your buildings happy. It was whilst working as part of this role that I had to visit Toxteth in Liverpool shortly after the riots. The severity of these can not be underplayed. There were burning buildings, over 1,000 police officers were engaged and over 300 were injured in the rioting.

The Toxteth environment was a collection of very attractive Georgian buildings that had been allowed to run into dilapidation. Community engagement was low. The houses had been converted into a series of bedsits, with very little social cohesion and the riot gave opportunities for people to display their dissatisfaction with their circumstances. In what could have been a beautiful environment there was poverty, social isolation and a complete lack of respect for the buildings that were destroyed, some of which were set fire to during the riots.

The engagement since the riots has rebuilt a community and secured that community's love and respect for their buildings.

Over my career I have seen increasing engagement by the community. As schools and media have influenced the understanding of the built environment, it has been much easier to communicate the vision for a new scheme and the long term plan for an area.

Translating a vision for the community has been revolutionised. I can still draw the shape and plan of Milton Keynes to explain it to people, and that's because we did this on a daily basis. The plan was used to describe a future to residents, to employers, to civic leaders, and to investors.

One of my favourite things when studying a town or city is to look at the old maps or old town plans. Today, with the benefit of technology, we can bring our vision for new developments to life so quickly and easily. Clippers Quay, a new Grainger project in the heart of Salford Quays, achieved great letting success using technology. The first phase was over 50% leased by the new residents prior to completion of construction. These new residents chose their home using virtual reality. This new technology has the power to enable us to walk down streets that will not be built for years, to sit in gardens that are not yet planted and to test our feelings on how they delight us. With the development of increasingly sophisticated software we can measure people's reaction to those new places.

At the end of 2015 I was appointed Chief executive of Grainger plc, the UK's largest listed residential landlord.

Grainger has the skills, knowledge and tenacity to take on long term challenging projects. We design at a building level in great detail but also can operate at a large scale. An example of this is the work we are doing with the Defence Infrastructure Organisation at Aldershot in Hampshire. Here we are taking a Victorian garrison town founded during the Crimean war and linking it back to create a vibrant urban extension of 370 acres using heritage buildings, landscaping, and our commitment to community engagement to ensure it is embraced by the local community. We are a 100 year old company designing and planning this community with the next 100 years in mind. The case study is summarised on page 80.

ALDERSHOT ENTERPRISE CENTRE

Wellesley, Aldershot in Hampshire – case study

SIZE AND SCALE	Transforming the former 370 acre Garrison into a new community which has identity as an urban expansion of Aldershot.
USES	850 new homes (35% affordable); refurbishment of six listed buildings; a new heritage trail providing access to historically significant monuments and memorials; two new primary schools; day care facilities; delivery of approximately 150 ha to SANGS ('Suitable Alternative Natural Green Space'), community and leisure facilities including a central park, new play areas, allotments, sports facilities; restoration and development of the canal frontage; a local centre with new offices and local shops, pub/restaurant; household waste recycling, and approximately 2.4 ha of employment area.
PARTNERS	Grainger plc, the Defence Infrastructure Organisation, and Rushmoor Borough Council.
TIMESCALES	Grainger selected as partner 2011, planning consent given 2014, first resident 2015, and first school 2018.
IMPACTS	As well as delivering a significant number of homes, schools and employment Wellesley will form a new area of Aldershot and will enhance the vitality of the town by opening up green spaces and leisure activity from a previously inaccessible area.
LOCATION	Wellesley is being developed to become a new area of Aldershot in Hampshire.
HISTORY OF THE SITE	Established in 1854, Aldershot Garrison became Britain's first purpose-built military base since Roman times, developed on both sides of the Basingstoke Canal. Aldershot went on to become known as the 'home of the British Army'. The pioneering Cambridge Military Hospital (CMH) is one of Aldershot's defining landmarks. After the hospital closed in 1996 and the British Army was reduced in size, the Garrison's South Camp gradually moved to new, more modern facilities in the North Camp. Rushmoor Borough Council began listing the significant Victorian buildings in 2001.
THE STRATEGY	To create a high quality sustainable extension to Aldershot. To build on the heritage and established pattern of streets to provide safe and permeable links to the town and enable residents of the wide community access to the green space. To build strong community relationships.
CHALLENGES TO DELIVERY	Ensuring that Wellesley was welcomed by and integrated with the wider Adlershot community. Bringing forward restoration of historic buildings, overcoming any negative perception of new build and property developers, and perceptions of a 'garrison town'. Remains of ordnance.
PROCUREMENT PROCESS	Public sector competitive tender process to select a master developer partner.

WELLESLEY: RESTORING THE 19TH CENTURY SMITH DORRIEN AS A COMMUNITY BUILDING

WELLESLEY: NEW HOUSING BENEFITING FROM MATURE LANDSCAPING AND REFLECTING HISTORIC MATERIALS

At Grainger, enriching people's lives through the quality of their homes and the quality of our service is at the heart of what we do. Around 98% of all landlords in the UK have less than ten properties and cannot replicate in design and service what Grainger is creating. The buildings we are creating are for the long term in the design and the way we manage them. We design in spaces for residents to meet and interact from lounge areas, gyms, and open terraces. We even give careful consideration to the way they collect their post.

In all buildings with over 100 flats we have on-site managers able to respond immediately to resident's queries. They also organise socials and quiz nights, book clubs or homework clubs in our family friendly homes. This is designed to encourage people to build friendships, to stay and put down roots and to talk proudly of their home and their community. It is for this reason we also offer longer leases to give people a sense of security whether it is commercial or residential or civic buildings. This combination of design and service will be critical to sustaining an area.

As I write this we are around the time that the country is due to leave the European Union. Two things are essential for the country to flourish and survive. One is to increase our productivity and the second is to restore pride and commitment in our country and in our built environments. Whilst many people cannot agree on things, a recent MORI poll discovered that there was one thing that eight out of ten people polled did agree on, and that was that the UK has a housing crisis.

In our ambition as a country to solve the housing crisis it is going to be evermore important that the solutions we build have a very clear vision and long term resilience, as good quality housing schemes are planned with people at the heart of them. Development will need to be respectful of all of the lessons learnt, and of our heritage, to ensure we are building a sustainable and resilient country for the future.

PRINCIPLES FOR A HUMAN CITY

DAVID PARTRIDGE

DAVID PARTRIDGE

David joined Argent Group PLC in 1990 and was appointed Joint Chief Executive in September 2006. He is now Managing Partner of Argent (Property Development) Services LLP and Executive Chairman of Argent Related.

He is a member of the Royal Institute of British Architects and a fellow of the Royal Society of British Sculptors. After a degree in architecture at Cambridge, he became a founding partner of Gebler Tooth Partridge Architects based in Chiswick.

In his current role at Argent David has overall responsibility for structuring and establishing financial and management programmes including for Argent's Related business. His responsibility covers major projects including King's Cross as well as all new projects. David also specifically oversees masterplanning, building design, financing, and all legal work.

He is Chairman of the Trustees of the UK GBC and Vice President of the British Property Federation.

Today, any visitor to King's Cross will discover a place which has been truly transformed. As well as being home to 1,500 people who live there and 15,000 people who work there (both of which will double as the scheme completes its final phases), over 15m visitors every year enjoy the many cultural and leisure attractions. This includes shops, 50 restaurants and bars, and the multiple events and activities which are hosted in the 25 acres of public open space and in the arts and cultural institutions housed there, such as Central St Martins, the House of Illustration, the Aga Khan Foundation, and the Everyman Cinema. This figure is also set to double with the opening of the Coal Drops Yard, more retail and restaurant outlets, and a new 600-person theatre still to be completed.

If they arrived there by time capsule from the end of the 20th Century, they would have been especially surprised, as in 2000, when Argent won the opportunity to become the Master Developer for the site, King's Cross was an area to be avoided, a place of destitution, prostitution, and drugs. How did this transformation come about?

In 2001, before setting pencil to paper on the first draft of the masterplan for the redevelopment of the 67 acre King's Cross Central site, Argent published a document entitled "Principles for a Human City". We set out ten principles to guide the way in which we intended to develop this new piece of city and we asked that everything that we did at King's Cross should be judged in accordance with them – not just in terms of the masterplan, which we would use as a framework for that development but also with regard to the long term success of the built project.

These principles were derived from Argent's experience of bringing forward the regeneration of Brindleyplace in Birmingham (since 1993), and from the lessons that we were learning in Manchester, where we had just embarked on the redevelopment of Piccadilly Gardens, in time for the 2002 Commonwealth Games.

A lot of attention has been focused on the Principles themselves, but it is interesting that (though none of us consciously realised this at the time) they were essentially founded in the idea of what a Human city should be - concepts which are set out in the Humanist Manifesto III published in 2003 as a successor to the first Humanist Manifesto of 1933, that:

- Knowledge of the world is derived from observation, experimentation and rational analysis;

- Humans are an integral part of nature, the result of evolutionary change;

- Ethical values are derived from human need and interest as tested by experience;

- Life's fulfilment emerges from individual participation in the service of humane ideals;

- Humans are social by nature and find meaning in relationships;

- Working to benefit society maximises individual happiness.

I first read these concepts many years later, in Steven Pinker's interpretation of Humanism (in his 2018 publication "Enlightenment Now"). Without in any way getting into the religious dimension or debate which has surrounded the Humanist movement, Argent's approach to delivering a successful built environment accords closely with these ideals.

I believe that successful and sustainable cities are those which can evolve in a natural way, are responsive to human need, can deliver societal benefit and provide meaning to all of the citizens who use them. We need to create cities which people can enjoy with pride. This belief probably comes from my own personal journey, following my father around from his time as a tea planter in Sri Lanka, where I was born, to Kerala and East Africa, where he exported tea, and then finally to Canada, where he attempted to import it. As a young child I would fly back to a UK boarding school and then attended the King's School, Canterbury going on to read Architecture at Christ's College, Cambridge. Everywhere I travelled, I was (in a sense) an outsider, always looking to work out how to get under the skin of the place in order to fit in. I took this curiosity and survival technique with me to Birmingham, to Manchester, and eventually to London.

The 10 principles for a human city

The Principles were essentially divided into two categories:

1   The What?

- A robust urban framework
- A lasting new place
- A vibrant mix of uses
- Work for King's Cross, work for London

2   The How?

- Harness the value of heritage
- Promote accessibility
- Commit to long-term success
- Engage and inspire
- Communicate clearly and openly
- Secure delivery

With the exception of substituting the relevant place/city in the fourth bullet, I believe that these principles could and should be converted into a credo to be applied to every city-making development project, and we continue to apply them to everything that we do, for instance to our next major regeneration project at Brent Cross South through Argent Related.

Human cities – what?

Central to the concept of creating successful places, is the idea that the fundamentals of a sustainable "masterplan" are not about stringing together a group of individual buildings, or even anchor uses but rather are about the laying down (hopefully for perpetuity) of an urban framework of streets and squares; known to us in the real estate industry as "public realm" but seen by the public as the open spaces through which they navigate and engage with the essence of a city.

In most western cities, it is this **robust urban framework** which has historically forged the character and personality of the place – often derived from early origins, in classical and then medieval incarnations, and then through explosive expansion in the 18th and 19th centuries. Positive examples of the impact of interventions in the making of a city are the Cerda grid in Barcelona (instigated in 1856), Baron von Haussman's re-modelling of Paris during the same period and Nash's elegant insertion of Regent's Street into London completed earlier, in 1825.

20th Century city planning was generally not so successful and post the Second World War most UK cities were designed from a perspective which put the automobile and economic efficiency at the forefront, much to the detriment of the cities themselves and of the humans who were the unfortunate and ungrateful subjects of this approach.

Argent have always led with the idea that public realm should be the first element in the delivery of any development, setting out the underlying grid of infrastructure over which every building would be accessed and serviced, thinking carefully about spatial hierarchy, variety and routes (for pedestrians and vehicles), and especially linking into surrounding assets and street patterns.

At Brindleyplace, in Birmingham, the main square was set out before any of the buildings around it were commissioned. This allowed it to become an address in its own right, which made it easier to attract office occupiers as they felt that they were moving into a completed piece of city rather than a building site. The case study is summarised on page 90.

Similarly, at Piccadilly Gardens and Piccadilly Place in Manchester the main public spaces were completed at the same time as the initial phases. At King's Cross over £450m has been invested into infrastructure, which has always run well ahead of the completion rate of the buildings themselves.

The urban framework became the skeleton around which the individual parts of the city are evolved, with the people that move through it providing the life-blood that brings the place alive.

This pattern of streets and squares is the essence of a **lasting new place** – one which will outlive the buildings themselves, and stand as a legacy for the future. Truly sustainable places however have to go beyond the physicality of the built environment. They have to assume a personality or a character which will register them within the psychic geography of a city – a destination which people want to visit and discover again and again.

The beautiful hard and soft landscaping at King's Cross, the parks, play spaces and the opening up of the canal-side to become a place which people flock to in all seasons, all contribute to the attraction of the public space. Just as Piccadilly Gardens is a rare and (over) popular piece of greenery in the bustling centre of Manchester, King's Cross provides a variety of different spaces and approaches to planting, to play – places to sit or walk, to picnic or to run and cycle, or just to watch the world go by in the city or on the canal.

Equally fundamental to creating a place which will stand out in the mind of citizens is a **vibrant mix of uses** – taking in not just places to work, live or shop, but also being open to accommodating everything else that a city should offer. This includes places to entertain and to be entertained, places to educate and to be educated, places that offer art, culture, music, food and drink for all tastes and all pockets, as well as places which provide space to breathe and rest within the bustling city life, and which provide basic amenities for all to prosper. Places which can delight and inspire.

Fundamental to this mix, is the idea of providing a **diversity of activity** and experience for everyone – young and old and from all backgrounds. From being the sponsors of the King's Cross Academy (a two form entry primary school, co-located with the Frank Barnes School for Deaf Children) through to staffing our KX Recruit office (which has just helped its 1000th person into employment, 70% from Camden or Islington), King's Cross has focused on providing opportunity for both the existing community and the new one we are creating.

BRINDLEYPLACE, CENTRAL SQUARE

Brindleyplace, Birmingham – case study

SIZE AND SCALE	£0.5bn GDV, 150,000 sq.m. floorspace across 17 acre site.
USES	Mixed use, 10,000 sq.m. of commercial space, 500 sq.m. retail, 250 new homes.
INFRASTRUCTURE	40% of the site is open, publically accessible space, accessible via 2 new canal bridges.
PARTNERS	Argent and Hermes, via the Argent Development Consortium.
TIMESCALES	1993-2004
IMPACTS	Complete regeneration of the canal side area, west of the International Convention Centre (ICC) as part of the Convention Quarter.
LOCATION	Between the ICC and the National Indoor Arena (NIA) bounded by the canal and Broad Street, Westside of Birmingham's city centre.
HISTORY OF THE SITE	The land was designated for mixed use as part of the Highbury Initiative, originally taken up by Rosehaugh. Argent stepped into their shoes after they went into administration in 1993.
THE STRATEGY	Forge links into the existing city centre and build out streets and spaces early, financed by early site sales – residential and the Sealife Centre.
CHALLENGES TO DELIVERY	Significant infrastructure requirements and credibility issue within the market as a new, untested area.
PROCUREMENT PROCESS	Open market bid to Rosehaugh's administrator.

BRINDLEYPLACE BEFORE REDEVELOPMENT

BRINDLEYPLACE AFTER REDEVELOPMENT

So much of late 20th Century planning policy drove urban design into mono-cultural zoning, often connected by the car. Long lasting places instead demand the highest degree of variety possible, not just to attract city-goers to today's cities but also to be flexible and resilient over time, as we are essentially creating platforms for people and businesses, let alone technologies which have not yet been invented.

We adopted this approach at Argent after extensive research into other developments of the mid to late 1990s from all around the world – from Broadgate and Canary Wharf in London to Potsdammer Platz in Berlin and Battery Park City in New York. Each of these suffered from being dominated by one particular use, or from being designed as a series of individual buildings with the spaces between them "left over" and unplanned – dominated by servicing or vehicles.

At the same time as working for the locality in which it is rooted, a truly successful place must also be capable of being attractive to a far wider audience. That is why King's Cross needed **to work for itself and to work for London** – and indeed for the UK as a whole, as it has increasingly appealed to an international audience of visitors arriving on the Eurostar and from further afield. The case study is summarised on page 94.

Human cities – how?

At the heart of creating a human city is the need to seek out the true "genus loci" of the place, either by looking back and harnessing the value of its history or by creating a new one, and often a bit of both is required for a place to feel authentic. The rich pattern of a place can become evident from its uses over hundreds of years, and the various activities which have occurred there. Often its very name is derived from what went on there. Piccadilly, for instance comes from a term used to describe a part of a garment made by the many tailors who worked in that location centuries earlier, and of course King's Cross is named after the crossing of streets on which a monument to King George IV once stood.

Re-inventing and re-purposing a place for a true re-incarnation can seek inspiration from what came before by highlighting and celebrating that history but at the same time it must not necessarily be a slavish pastiche. Often a completely new approach will be required to rejuvenate an area or a building for a new future.

At King's Cross the re-use of the four gasholders to provide new homes (by Wilkinson Eyre) and a public park (by Bell Phillips), and the re-invention of the Coal Drops Yard (by Thomas Heatherwick) as the new future of experiential retail are great examples, alongside the Granary building conversion (by Stanton Williams) for Central St Martins and Granary Square itself (by Robert Townshend Landscape Architects) of how to truly "**harness the value of heritage**".

It is not enough however, just to bring historical buildings and unloved areas of city back into re-use if no one is encouraged to rediscover them and enjoy them. So **promoting accessibility** and permeability throughout any new master-planned regeneration scheme is absolutely vital.

New streets and squares will help people to move around but they will never be sufficiently populated if no one can get there in the first place. Firstly, public transport is essential and secondly, links into any new, improved or existing infrastructure are necessary to ensure the free flow of footfall.

Argent built a new pedestrian bridge into Brindleyplace from the International Convention Centre, similarly from Piccadilly Station into Piccadilly Place in Manchester, and two new canal bridges at King's Cross, as well as ensuring that the framework of movement within our development sites picked up, matched and enhanced existing street patterns wherever possible. At Brent Cross South, a key element will be a new Thameslink Station, anchoring one end of the masterplan.

But accessibility is not just about physical links, it is also about an attitude to how a place is managed, who is encouraged to enjoy it and what sort of behaviours are tolerated within that area. All of the roads which we have built in Birmingham, Manchester and London have been to adoptable standards and all of the spaces that we have created have maintained an open and inviting approach to all users, with exceptions only for criminal or publicly offensive behaviour. People from all demographics and all walks of life can enjoy those spaces, and indeed feel an ownership of them and emotional connection to them.

KING'S CROSS, GRANARY SQUARE

King's Cross Central, London N1C – case study

SIZE AND SCALE	£3.5 billion GDV, 800,000 sq.m. floorspace across 67 acre site.
USES	Mixed use, 400,000 sq.m. of commercial space, 5,000 sq.m retail, 1,500 sq.m arts, cultural, education and leisure and 2,000 new homes.
INFRASTRUCTURE	25 acres of new high-quality public realm delivering 20 new streets and 10 squares and parks.
PARTNERS	The King's Cross Central Partnership comprises the Australian Superannuation Fund (Aus Super), the BT Pension Scheme and Argent.
TIMESCALES	2000-2025.
IMPACTS	Over 35,000 jobs with occupiers such as Google, Deep Minds, Facebook, Universal Music and Havas; 2 new primary schools, 2 universities (the Aga Khan Foundation and Central St Martins); circa 40% affordable housing, a 600 seat cinema, over 50 restaurants, shops, sports and community facilities, significant re-purposing of heritage assets all generating thousands of visitors.
LOCATION	Centred around the derelict Goods Yard and the Regent's Canal, between King's Cross and St Pancras stations.
HISTORY OF THE SITE	The King's Cross Railway Lands had been falling into disuse and disrepute since the 1980's, and two previous attempts at regeneration had failed, before the re-routing of Phase 2 of the Channel Tunnel Rail Link (now HS1) into St Pancras became the catalyst for the Argent King's Cross Partnership (AKXLP) to join with the landowners LCR and DHL in 2000 to promote a new scheme. Planning permission was granted in 2006 and the development began in earnest in November 2007.
THE STRATEGY	Argent (as developer) spent the early 2000's masterplanning and achieving planning permission for the site. In 2008, the Landowners agreed to retain a 50% stake in the development (exiting in 2016 when selling their stake to Aus Super), allowing Argent to concentrate on re-cycling early capital disposals into building out the infrastructure and public realm, which serviced the individual plots.
CHALLENGES TO DELIVERY	Significant infrastructure requirements (c£450m) compounded by market disruption from 2008 recession.
PROCUREMENT PROCESS	Competitive bid won by Argent St George in 2000, subsequently taken on by Argent through AKXLP.

KING'S CROSS BEFORE REDEVELOPMENT

KINGS'S CROSS AFTER REDEVELOPMENT

Equally important in successfully following through this sort of approach to creating human cities is a **commitment to long-term success**, which allows owners, developers and investors (and in Argent's case we are all three of those in one) to take a view beyond the most immediate return. Linking this approach with the diverse range of uses at our employ can create a mix of activity and occupiers, which can mature and evolve over time, rather than being driven by a need to maximise cash returns and/or covenant strength in order to affect a quick sale.

Having the BT Pension Scheme and the Australian Superannuation Fund as long term partners and investors, the former providing vital patient money in the early years of all of Argent's developments, has been critical in shaping the eventual outcome of places which have been designed to generate long term income and value for all. King's Cross has (flatteringly) been described as the next great London Estate, after those owned by the historic landowners in the West End – such as the Crown, the Grosvenor, Portman, and Howard de Walden.

PANORAMIC VIEW OF KING'S CROSS

The key ingredient required to turn this vision into reality, alongside endless patience and commitment, is the ability to **engage and inspire** at every level of the stakeholder spectrum – from national, regional and local politicians and officers to the communities which will become part of the regeneration story; from investors, financiers and occupiers to people who will buy the homes that we create, to those who will enjoy the shopping and lifestyle choices on offer. **Clear and open communication** and, above all, an ability to articulate and relate a story about the vision which we have, has been crucial in demonstrating the conviction that is needed to navigate these multi-phased projects through to fruition.

Equally important is the formation of Local Partnerships, which Argent founded for Broad Street in Birmingham, for the Piccadilly Area in Manchester, and for King's Cross and St Pancras in London. These provided a way to pull together those businesses and people who are already invested in the local area to maximise benefits, harmonise policy and influence wider outcomes.

These partnerships brought together organisations and businesses which shared a common investment in their particular locality and which were able to act together in a private capacity (although their natural evolution is one day to become Business Improvement Districts as Broad Street did) in order to progress an agenda of street improvement, activity and CSR. All of these Partnerships now have their own life – Piccadilly Partnership in Manchester and the Urban Partners in King's Cross – and are driven by local stakeholders for the benefit of the people who live and work well beyond the "red line" of Argent's original investment.

Finally, all of this is wonderful only in theory unless the teams promoting the story have the ability to **secure delivery**, and let actions speak louder than words. It has always been an Argent mantra to "under-promise and over-deliver". Having steadfast long term backers and trusted finances is crucial to carrying the conviction through to reality – and this will be continued in all of Argent's future projects through our partnership with the Related Companies from the USA.

How is success measured?

It is easy to look back at pictures of children playing happily in fountains and feel good about the place that has been created but the true test of the success of any development must be the long-term value which has been created for everyone who has been touched by it.

In 2017, Argent commissioned Regeneris to look back at 10 years of physical development at King's Cross and to assess its impact against a number of different criteria. Firstly they looked at how much had been achieved against each of the ten original principles – set out overleaf:

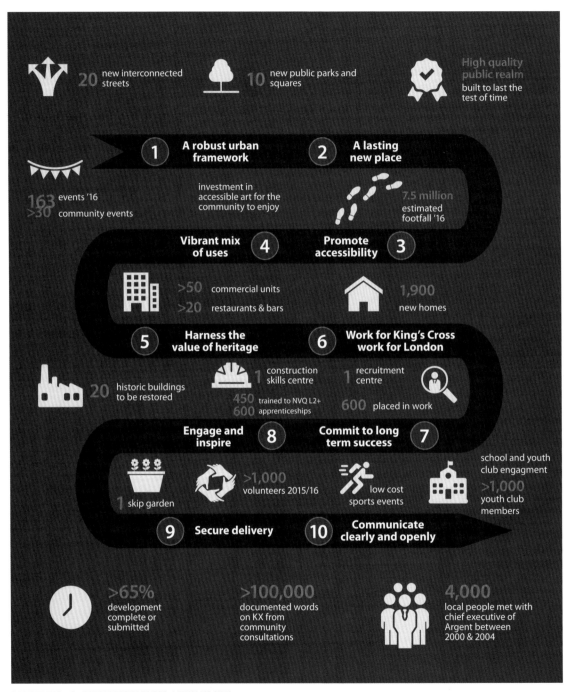

20 new interconnected streets

10 new public parks and squares

High quality public realm built to last the test of time

1 A robust urban framework

2 A lasting new place

163 events '16
>30 community events

investment in accessible art for the community to enjoy

7.5 million estimated footfall '16

4 Vibrant mix of uses

3 Promote accessibility

>50 commercial units
>20 restaurants & bars

1,900 new homes

5 Harness the value of heritage

6 Work for King's Cross work for London

20 historic buildings to be restored

1 construction skills centre
450 trained to NVQ L2+
600 apprenticeships

1 recruitment centre
600 placed in work

8 Engage and inspire

7 Commit to long term success

1 skip garden
>1,000 volunteers 2015/16
low cost sports events

school and youth club engagment
>1,000 youth club members

9 Secure delivery

10 Communicate clearly and openly

>65% development complete or submitted

>100,000 documented words on KX from community consultations

4,000 local people met with chief executive of Argent between 2000 & 2004

DELIVERING AGAINST PRINCIPLES FOR A HUMAN CITY

The results speak for themselves. We also asked them to assess actual value created in a number of areas:

- Value of construction spend
- Homes created (and different tenures)
- Jobs created, including through local Construction Training and the KX Recruit initiative
- Placemaking
- Community

We firmly believe that applying metrics such as these, especially to the latter two categories, are essential in order to analyse and demonstrate the true impact of development and to encourage an approach which brings in wider societal and environmental sustainable practices alongside purely financial driven outcomes.

THE ECONOMIC, SOCIAL AND FINANCIAL FOOTPRINT OF KING'S CROSS: A SNAPSHOT

Human cities – why?

It is only by holding oneself up to this sort of measurement and scrutiny that the real estate sector can hope to become seen as part of the solution to the schisms in society which have provided such earth rendering political disruption in the decade since the great crash of 2008, rather than being perceived as part of the problem.

Regardless of political persuasion, it is commonly perceived that there is a gulf opening up between the haves and the have-nots, between those who have benefitted from the magnetic pull of people into cities and the progress of those cities versus those who feel left behind or squeezed out by gentrification (though this feeling does not stand up to scientific analysis at all as Steven Pinker so persuasively pointed out in his aforementioned book).

It is incumbent on those of us who do believe that it is possible to create better lives through better places, to set out our philosophical approach and to have it tested accordingly – and then to absorb and adapt for future ventures.

Human cities – who?

This theoretical approach would stay as such if it wasn't for the work of a number of key individuals in the UK, who have been pioneering and practising place-based development for the last 20 years – many of them are co-authors of chapters in this book.

Private sector entrepreneurship must be matched by outstanding civic leadership with brave and committed politicians and officers prepared to espouse and execute the views that I have set out here. There is a need to think long term, to encourage partnerships and to foster success through the understanding of mutual alignments in order to create win-win outcomes.

Argent brings together a whole host of people with different backgrounds, from planning engineering, financial, legal, design and management, in order to effect this sort of transformative, "good" development (as described by the Mayor of London).

My own training is, I believe, also critically influential. I always feel that an architect's job is to bring together the sometimes seemingly irreconcilable demands of the brief, the regulations, the budget and gravity together into an elegant and timeless solution, always seeking out the highest common factors rather than falling back on the lowest common denominators. This seems to me to define Argent's approach too.

Can cities be human?

So how well does the reality match up to the theory. Indeed is it possible to create human cities which match the criteria set out by the Humanist Manifesto III?

- Knowledge of the world/cities is derived from observation, experimentation and rational analysis:

  The approach I have espoused is entirely based on analysis of successful urban approaches through the ages, and indeed of current practice (for instance at Msheireb in Doha). A scientifically sound approach to measurement along the lines which has been described, will allow us to both look back at the real value(s) which our activities have generated and look forward to assess and anticipate future propositions and to adjust or adapt them accordingly.

- Humans/cities are an integral part of nature, the result of evolutionary change:

  The "framework" based approach to master-planning and regeneration allows for change and adaption over time. The streets and squares, parks, canals and connections which are fundamental to laying out cities have every chance of being in place for millennia, whereas the buildings may not last as long, or will be adapted and re-purposed in themselves over time.

- Ethical values are derived from human need and interest as tested by experience:

  Especially in this age of social media, cities are all about experience and a human approach to combining those values with meaning through places where increasingly the majority of humanity will live, is essential to making cheek-by-jowl life in ever higher density conglomerations ethical. Only through forging a pattern of city making which places human values at the forefront, will we be able to truly densify and intensify habitation in such a way as to deliver the much needed environmental sustainability and carbon neutrality that such clustering can create.

- Life's fulfilment emerges from individual participation in the service of humane ideals and humans are social by nature and find meaning in relationships through cities:

  Without such an approach, everyday life in cities will be dominated by an aggressive environment of over-crowding, of pollution combined with competition and loneliness – it is of paramount importance that we create places which can provide the opportunity to encourage purpose and pride.

Through this philosophy we can create cities which work to benefit society and thus maximise individual happiness.

A final word

Taken from the Humanist Manifesto III:

> "Humanists are concerned for the well-being of all, are committed to diversity, and respect those of differing yet humane views. We work to uphold the equal enjoyment of human rights and civil liberties in an open, secular society and to maintain it is a civic duty to participate in the democratic process and a planetary duty to protect nature's integrity, diversity, and beauty in a secure, sustainable manner".

Argent's approach to city-making seeks to put this into practice on every level. Our purpose is to Take Pride of Place, and we do this by taking pride in:

- Delivering on our promises together;

- Shaping inspirational and enduring places; and

- Creating a valuable legacy for all.

THE IMPORTANCE OF COLLABORATION

SIR EDWARD LISTER

SIR EDWARD LISTER

Sir Edward is Chairman of Homes England, the Government's Housing Agency. He is also an Advisor to the Department of International Trade on Capital Investment and a Non Executive Director of the Foreign and Commonwealth Office.

In 2011 Sir Edward was knighted for services to Local Goverment.

Formerly Sir Edward was Chief of Staff to the Mayor of London Boris Johnson and Deputy Mayor of Policy and Planning from 2011 to 2016. Prior to that Sir Edward was Leader of Wandsworth Borough Council for 19 years (1992 to 2011) making him one of the longest serving Council Leaders in the country. Sir Edward has served on the London Legacy Development Corporation from 2011 to 2016, set up and was first Chairman of the Old Oak Common Mayoral Development Corporation (2014 to 2016) and Chairman of London and Partners, the London inward investment agency (2013 to 2016).

Sir Edward's achievements in regeneration have been recognised in 2011 by being made a Freeman of the London Borough of Wandsworth, in 2014 achieving the London First London Award, and in that same year the Estates Gazette London Award. He is also a Freeman of the City of London.

I came into public service to make a real difference. I cared about my home, my family, and my community. Wandsworth is where I grew up, where my children went to school, and where I met my wife. I found my borough fascinating and frustrating. There was such variety, inequality, and untapped potential. Smart Victorian streets sat next to failing high rise council estates. There were wide open commons, beautiful civic buildings, and rundown town centres. Some people prospered and some were left behind. I wanted to make things better for everyone and that's what first led me to the town hall.

In 1976 I was fortunate to join a council with strong civic leaders and with a real sense of purpose. I was an opposition back bencher and the Leader of the day was Cllr Tony Belton. I disagreed with his policies but I admired the passion and energy he brought to the debate. On my own benches I was most impressed by Cllr Paul Beresford (now Sir Paul Beresford MP) and I shared his vision for a more dynamic, open and aspirational borough.

I learnt very early on that local authorities could not manage every challenge by themselves. They would have to adapt and find new ways of working if they were to drive positive change and create a more successful community.

What was true when I started out is no less relevant today. My career in public service has always been driven by the search for new solutions. How to attract investment, how to make the best of existing resources of land and people, and how to deliver results for communities.

Today, my focus is on unlocking land, releasing difficult sites for development, and achieving national targets for new homes. It requires persistence, ingenuity, and a readiness on the part of all agencies in all sectors to work together and seek common solutions. There is no other way.

A new approach in Wandsworth

When I was first elected to Wandsworth Council in the 1970's it was a badly rundown borough. Much of the private sector housing was in poor condition and lacking basic amenities. The vast high-rise council housing estates which dominated large areas of Battersea and Roehampton suffered from chronic underinvestment. Even the smaller cottage estates were in decline.

The Thames riverside from Wandsworth to Nine Elms was a tangle of industrial sites, many of them coming to the end of their uses. Battersea Power Station, still producing electricity for London at this stage, was the most prominent building on this landscape.

The borough was blessed with many parks, commons and green open spaces – but these too had become tired, unloved, and in some cases unsafe. The town centres of Putney, Wandsworth Town, Clapham Junction, Balham, and Tooting were dying on their feet as people moved out of the inner city in search of better quality housing and a more welcoming environment.

This was the challenge that the newly-elected Wandsworth Council faced in May 1978. We wanted quite simply to restore local people's pride in their borough – and to make it a place where people wanted to live, work, and bring up their families. As a young councillor I was determined to play my part in this transformation and I was fortunate to secure my first front bench role as Chair of the Leisure and Amenities Committee. We started by addressing the basic local services which are essential to a decent quality of life. We tackled street cleaning, refuse collection, and parks and highways maintenance. We launched what was to become a council-wide programme of market-testing – ensuring that services were properly specified before being exposed to competition.

Unsurprisingly, this approach – radical at the time – generated fierce opposition from some quarters. We were characterised as ideologues. In fact, our only dogma was to insist on delivering the best services for our residents at the best price. So while many services were outsourced, others remained in-house as staff-led teams competed successfully with their private sector competitors.

What drove us was a simple desire to get the best value from local services, and in doing so, give our residents a positive reason to live in our borough. This meant getting the best from our existing workforce while attracting new private sector contractors that could bring their own energy and expertise to Wandsworth. This was the beginning of a public and private sector partnership that was key to driving up standards - laying secure and lasting foundations for the long-term regeneration of the whole borough.

None of this was easy and as pioneers we made our fair share of mistakes but over time Wandsworth became a better place for everyone, whether you lived in a leafy residential area or a high-rise estate. Today, this common sense, pragmatic approach to service delivery has become widespread throughout the public sector and is far less likely to arouse political controversy as the practices we championed in the 1970's and 1980's. The following pages attempt to unpick some of these changes and show how they continue to influence my thinking around place-making and the value of partnership.

The foundations for growth

In Wandsworth, the policy of market testing soon developed beyond traditional blue collar areas to white collar services. Some of the biggest savings were in previously untested back office functions. The scale of our ambition meant that very soon we were generating substantial savings, which could be used both to reduce the burden of local taxation for our residents and to increase investment in local amenities.

Our approach to asset management, which really came of age while Sir Paul Beresford was Leader, was rigorous and delivered substantial capital receipts. These funds underpinned four decades of investment in council housing, schools, libraries, parks, commons, and local streets. We famously upgraded our street lighting, which was noticeable as soon as you entered the borough at night. It gave rise to the 'brighter borough' brand that the council is still known by today.

We prioritised investment in the major commons in Wandsworth and Tooting, as well as other small parks and public gardens, creating a more inviting and family-friendly environment. Following the dissolution of the Greater London Council, Wandsworth took over Battersea Park and spent £1m, a huge sum at the time, transforming it from a crime hotspot into a well maintained, secure and welcoming place.

HOW BATTERSEA PARK LOOKS TODAY

These changes had a profound effect on people's quality of life, making the borough the safe, welcoming place it is today. They restored local pride and established the council's reputation as a forward-thinking, well-run authority with a positive attitude to the private sector. This in turn created the low-tax environment that generations of Wandsworth residents have come to associate with their local council.

By setting a distinctively low council tax rate, we could leave our residents with more money in their pockets – and by investing in town centres and supporting local businesses the council could encourage people to spend locally. Ultimately, this open, business-friendly approach created the environment which has made the borough so attractive to external investors.

From planners to regenerators

Planning has always fascinated me. It can be contentious and confrontational in the short-term but places with ambitious, long-term strategies are far more likely to improve and thrive. In Wandsworth, we knew that our local planning framework was the key to really transforming local life. It had to be clear, deliverable and offer a compelling vision that investors would believe in.

So we set about relaxing local policies as a means of encouraging a greater variety of planning uses. This in turn led to an upsurge in the private sector provision of new schools, nurseries and leisure facilities – accelerating the pace of change in the borough and further increasing its attractiveness to other potential investors.

We worked hard to develop an open and responsive culture within the planning service itself. We made sure planning officers understood exactly what we wanted in our primary regeneration areas, and empowered them to give unambiguous, clear advice. It was their job to make good development happen and to broker solutions when plans hit problems.

This was a significant cultural change for the planning service but the officers welcomed it. They wanted to make good things happen and Wandsworth quickly became known as the best place for an aspirational planner to come and work.

Alongside our open planning department, we shaped a proactive economic development service, with a mandate to sell our vision and attract the private capital to make it happen. We saw attracting new investment to our regeneration areas as a core council function, not an optional extra or something that could be left to chance.

We knew we had to start with the large swathes of failing industrial land on the Thames riverside. Here lay the greatest challenges. One of the first breakthroughs came on the former Morgan Crucible factory site just west of Battersea Bridge. We managed to secure an attractive low-rise private residential development. Completed in 1984, the new homes were built alongside a new riverside walk and public square. The outcome changed people's perceptions of the Battersea riverside and its industrial past.

Now more landowners and investors began to see the potential of such sites and they found a planning service that was very much open for business. Having become Council Leader, I played an active promotional role, advancing the borough's cause at every opportunity. We raced all over London to talk up Wandsworth and I had an open door policy so any investors could meet face-to-face to talk through their plans. At all times we were clear about what we wanted, negotiated in good faith and never went back on an agreement.

This formula served us well, and more of Wandsworth's industrial sites gave way to the residential and mixed use developments that now characterise the south bank of the Thames. One of our biggest wins was convincing the U.S. Embassy to relocate from Grosvenor Square to our Nine Elms regeneration area. This was a true game changer for this part of north Battersea and spurred the delivery of thousands of new jobs and homes.

I think we could do more to celebrate the role all levels of government play in securing inward investment and the social benefits that come with it. In many cases politicians are heavily criticised for doing this well, which is a real shame. In my experience the most successful places openly welcome private investment and we need to highlight the long-term benefits this brings to local communities and neighbourhoods.

Reviving council estates

Another key ingredient in Wandsworth's resurgence was the council's housing estate regeneration programme. By the mid-1980's, many post-war blocks were showing severe physical faults and design flaws. For example, the exceptionally long slab blocks of the Arndale estate in Wandsworth town centre had internal corridors running the full length of the building. These grim and oppressive tunnels were so long you could barely see the far end and were universally hated by all who lived there.

Other blocks were simply unfit for habitation. Thrown up quickly in the post-war years, they were damp, plagued with basic utility faults and impossible to keep warm. The older estates had little or no amenities, and offered hard landscapes cut off from the surrounding communities. These bleak environments gave rise to severe social problems and a great many homes were boarded up and abandoned. The case for change was clear and we were determined to act to ensure the borough worked for everyone who lived there.

Against this backdrop, the council decided to redevelop or release underused housing sites, offering existing residents superior homes in more attractive and welcoming settings. We reinvested the proceeds and created sustainable council estates. This active approach to managing council land allowed us to fund a borough-wide estate investment programme which dramatically improved the quality of life for our estate residents.

We upgraded scores of estates; redesigning poor performing buildings, installing double glazing, new kitchens and bathrooms, providing better amenities and investing more in cleaning, landscaping and maintenance. The estates could now be managed much more efficiently and became brighter and more successful places. In 2007, our estates were the first in the country to meet the Labour Government's decent homes standard. Not surprisingly, our estate residents soon posted the highest satisfaction scores in the social housing sector. Today, there are still boroughs where homes fail to meet this standard.

Fixing Wandsworth town centre

The revival of Wandsworth town centre offers one of the most significant examples of a successful public-private regeneration partnership. Stretched across two heavily congested sections of the South Circular Road, the area was dominated by the Arndale housing estate, a dated shopping centre, warehousing and industrial sites, ageing office blocks, a gasworks, and the 7.75 acre Ram Brewery site.

Tackling this web of historic planning challenges would require a collaborative approach with every public and private stakeholder pulling in the same direction. Things really got going here in the early 2000's, in large part through the creation of an influential Town Centre Partnership Board. This became the vehicle for shaping a shared and ambitious vision for the area. It included the main landowners and employers, as well as small businesses, resident and amenity groups, the council, and Transport for London, who manage the town centre road network.

The priorities identified by the partnership board were reflected in the council's emerging planning policy, creating a blueprint for the area's development which was actively supported and promoted by all the partners.

THOUSANDS OF HOMES HAVE BEEN BUILT ALONG THE WANDSWORTH RIVERSIDE

FORMER INDUSTRIAL SITES NOW OFFER AMENITIES AND OPEN SPACES

Kick-starting delivery took a mix of persuasion and direct intervention from the council. We started by addressing the severe design faults of the housing estate, splitting the enormous slab block into three distinct buildings. We worked with the shopping centre owners to create a new entrance from the High Street. As the shops and the housing improved, the operator was able to attract Waitrose to the rebranded Southside Shopping Centre, along with Cineworld, and a string of major retail and restaurant brands.

On the opposite side of the High Street, we collaborated with the owners of the now derelict Ram Brewery site to shape plans for a new pedestrian quarter with a mix of homes, restaurants, a microbrewery, landscaped riverbanks and a public square. The first new homes were completed here in 2018 and have quickly become established as part of a new and distinctive quarter in the heart of the town centre. To help finally resolve the area's long standing traffic issues we negotiated a major S106 contribution from the developer towards the cost of the area's redesign.

Transport for London now expects to start work to replace the old one-way system in 2021. This will complete the transformation of the town centre from a place once dominated by its traffic into a smart, welcoming location where people can live, shop and enjoy their leisure.

The Nine Elms story

The very north east tip of Wandsworth, was once an industrial powerhouse and major logistics centre. It was home to Battersea Power Station, New Covent Garden Market (the country's largest fresh produce wholesale market), the South London Royal Mail Distribution Centre and dozens of warehousing and industrial estates. Its decline can be traced back to the late 1970s, with the closure of Battersea Power Station coming a few years later.

What made Nine Elms so challenging was its sheer scale and complete lack of basic utilities and infrastructure. The vast majority of land was in private ownership and the enormous power station's Grade II* Listing (which the council supported) made that key site even more complex.

These difficulties were amplified by the district's physical isolation. The bulk of Nine Elms sits within a roughly shaped triangle, with its northern edge meeting the Thames and its two other sides defined by high railway viaducts which cut it off from the residential communities beyond. There were a few successful developments on the very fringes, as well as several doomed attempts to tackle the Power Station site but Nine Elms remained a largely underdeveloped and isolated landscape until the early 2000's.

At this time, London was growing and housing demand was on the rise. Taking the partnership model developed in Wandsworth town centre, we now began an ambitious, coordinated approach to regenerating Nine Elms and addressing its chronic lack of infrastructure.

Early proposals were for a new railway shuttle service between Battersea Park Station and Victoria, using existing track. This would give us the transport capacity to support a new residential community in Nine Elms but detailed studies ruled it out.

Next, came the idea of extending the Northern Line from Kennington to Nine Elms. This seemed a far-fetched prospect but in theory at least, it tackled the area's transport deficiency and would vastly increase development capacity right across the district. This proposal was developed by the power station's then owners, Treasury Holdings, and then supported by the charismatic Tan Sri Liew who would later buy the iconic site as part of a Malaysian consortium.

Our hope was that we could pay for the Tube link by applying a tariff to the large volume of development it would unlock across Nine Elms. With this approach in mind, we met the key landowners and public authorities involved, and began to build a consensus behind the project.

As our ambitions for Nine Elms grew, it became clear that a development of this scale could not end abruptly on the borough boundary. Neighbouring Vauxhall was very different to industrial Nine Elms but was already a regeneration priority for Lambeth Council and there was clear scope for an overarching masterplan. The benefits of joined-up working clearly outweighed the political differences between the two councils and we united behind the Northern Line Extension.

By 2008, the new Mayor of London Boris Johnson had moved into City Hall with a mandate to increase housing delivery. We made our pitch and he agreed to create the "Vauxhall, Battersea, Nine Elms Opportunity Area" within his first London Plan. Our high level target was for 16,000 homes and 25,000 jobs, but this level of development was contingent on the successful delivery of the Northern Line Extension, without which the area would grow to a much lower density.

The next key step was to commission a Development Infrastructure Funding Study (DIFS) to determine how much the landowners within the Opportunity Area could be expected to pay towards the new Tube link. The study established a set of development tariffs that could be pooled to form an area-wide infrastructure fund. This would later become the area's Community Infrastructure Levy regime.

Crucially, the tariff was not imposed on the area's landowners. Instead, we worked in partnership to build a consensus behind this approach. There was some scepticism but ultimately they agreed to participate in the funding study, and accepted higher infrastructure contributions in exchange for higher development density.

Even with the DIFS tariff we still couldn't afford to fully finance the Tube extension and other necessary community infrastructure, including a new NHS health centre, a public park, a new primary school and the expansion of an existing one. Our proposal for closing the funding gap was a Tax Incremental Financing (TIF) scheme.

In essence, our TIF committed future business rates income within the Opportunity Area towards paying for the Tube extension. This arrangement would last for 25 years, providing an increasing flow of revenue as all of the planned offices, shops, restaurants and other commercial spaces filled up with rate paying businesses.

This was a highly innovative model and would become the largest TIF scheme in UK history. We expected it to raise in the region of £2bn over the full 25 years – enabling us to fund the Northern Line Extension and the wider package of social infrastructure. Our key task was to convince the Treasury that our unique funding model could work, and we took every opportunity to set out the enormous benefits this tube link could deliver.

In 2012, the dam broke and the then Chancellor George Osborne's Autumn Budget confirmed that the Government would underwrite a £1bn loan for the Northern Line Extension. The Greater London Authority would borrow the money and then pay it back through a combination of our development tariffs and future business rates growth.

With the Tube extension now on solid ground, more local landowners moved into development-mode and the district is now on course to provide around 22,000 mixed tenure homes, 6,000 more than originally planned. The completed area will also be home to the tech giant Apple, the U.S. Embassy, a revived New Covent Garden Market, a fully restored Battersea Power Station and a Linear Park which sweeps through the district from east to west. All of this is being delivered through partnership, and at very low cost to the taxpayer.

London's Opportunity Areas

In 2011, I left Wandsworth Council to join City Hall as Deputy Mayor for Planning and Chief of Staff. This was just over halfway through Boris Johnson's first term as London Mayor, and my appointment followed the tragic death of Sir Simon Milton, who had been instrumental in reshaping the London Plan and establishing the city's Opportunity Areas.

London was still feeling the effects of the financial crisis and the housing delivery numbers were a long way below the pre-recession peak. Market confidence was still low, the public finances were very weak and we did not have the vast housing delivery budget today's administration has at its disposal.

THE NINE ELMS LANDSCAPE BEFORE ITS REGENERATION BEGAN

HOW THE REVIVED NINE ELMS DISTRICT IS SET TO LOOK

As I joined City Hall several of the Opportunity Areas were well into delivery. King's Cross, Nine Elms, the Olympic Park, and Woolwich had momentum and boots on the ground. Others, including Old Oak Common, Elephant and Castle, and City Fringe (now Tech City), were still in their infancy and had many hurdles yet to clear. With London's population on course to reach 10 million, my job was to help restore the feel good factor and bring more of these areas into production.

Until now City Hall's role in planning and development had been strategic and broadly regulatory, with London's 33 councils dealing directly with developers and driving progress at a local level. This worked well in boroughs with strong planning teams and a committed regeneration programme but could easily falter where the expertise or political will was not strong enough to push things forward at the pace required.

So the challenge for us at City Hall was to take a more proactive approach to increasing delivery, without undermining councils or giving them cause to turn against the Mayor's housing agenda. In other words, we needed to adopt a collaborative approach which struck a careful balance between challenge and support, ensuring the boroughs found our interventions helpful, not embarrassing.

Before we could put this into practice, we had to change the mind-set inside City Hall and make the planning team more accountable for delivery. Just as in Wandsworth three decades earlier, we told them they had to make things happen. We needed to inject a new sense of urgency in the way we approached development and to adopt the role of pragmatic problem solvers who could be counted on to lift barriers and open doors.

Thanks to a highly capable management team, led by Stuart Murray and Colin Wilson, this transition was swift, and we became far more adept at resolving tricky issues and enabling development. Each Opportunity Area called for different solutions. At Southall, we took the lead on land assembly and managed the CPO process for vital access sites around a vast redundant gasworks. This gave Ealing Council scope to develop plans for around 5,000 homes, alongside a new park and town centre.

At Elephant and Castle, we persuaded Transport for London to create new entrances to the Tube station, which previously could only be accessed via a chronically congested set of lifts. This provided the wider Opportunity Area the transport capacity it needed to grow, and gave Southwark Council's regeneration efforts fresh momentum.

At Barking Riverside there was plenty of good land but like so much of the Docklands, development was held back by poor access. Here, we engaged Transport for London and Network Rail, and after a false start, settled on electrifying an existing length of rail line and delivering a new stretch of track. This will give the Opportunity Area scope for more than 10,000 new homes and will realise Barking and Dagenham Council's long held ambition to electrify the Goblin Line.

Alongside this focussed work in the Opportunity Areas, City Hall took a far more active role in attracting inward investment. This was spearheaded by the Mayor, who travelled the globe showcasing London's potential. His profile opened doors which remained firmly shut to other city leaders, and he brought back major new investment from Europe, America and Canada, as well as opening up new markets in China, the Middle East and Far East.

We became far more open and engaged on the home front too, with the Mayor and I chairing monthly meetings with London's development industry and council leaders. These sessions were all about finding pragmatic solutions to the inevitable delivery challenges thrown up by major regeneration programmes. We found that providing a regular, strategic forum kept everyone focussed on the big picture and we managed to resolve many emerging conflicts before they could slow progress or cost money.

Similar sessions were held with London's key housing associations, and we made it our business to bring utility companies, government departments, transport authorities, banks and passive landowners to the negotiating table. We made better use of City Hall's influence and soft power, and the more time and energy we invested in our networks, the more effective and ambitious we became.

We worked with UK Trade and Investment, as well as Hackney, Islington and Newham Councils, to drive international investment at Tech City and create a thriving new home for the digital economy. We worked with Camden Council to establish MedCity at King's Cross as a new global hub for medical research and life sciences, centred on the remarkable Francis Crick Institute. We brokered a deal with the Ministry of Sound to get homes built on a neighbouring site with exceptional acoustic protection. In short, we helped out everywhere we could, anyway we could, so long as it moved London in the right direction.

During my spell at City Hall, the number of new homes delivered each year went from just below 22,000, to more than 30,000. The number rose to 39,000 the following year as the developments we set in train continued to deliver. London had become an even greater, more diverse and welcoming world city, and vast swathes of brownfield land had made way for exciting new uses and new communities. This delivery record is testament to strong partnership working, and was achieved despite a 10 per cent cut in the Mayor's tax rate, the financial crisis and a dramatic decrease in Government funding.

A national role at Homes England

After leaving City Hall in 2016, I joined the Homes and Communities Agency (HCA) as Chairman. By this time, the organisation had been through a series of mergers, reinventions and spending reviews, and it bore many scars. It had become an awkward hybrid, part grant-giving body, part brownfield regeneration agency, part social housing regulator. An interim chief executive was holding the reigns and wherever you looked, you found a square peg in a round hole. It was no longer the organisation that had come into force in 2008 and helped keep housebuilding going in the face of the global downturn.

My initial brief from the-then Communities Secretary Greg Clarke was to rebuild the agency's capacity and get its various growth and housing programmes up to speed. As the Government's housing agenda developed over the next year, plans for the future role of the HCA became more tightly focussed on accelerating homebuilding. What ministers realised, as did I, was the need for a dealmaker that could stimulate real change in the market and ensure more public land was not only released but shepherded through the planning process and into delivery.

So in January 2018, we officially relaunched the HCA as Homes England, with a much sharper focus on accelerating housing delivery. We had a new chief executive, Nick Walkley, with significant experience of reshaping public service bodies, and a new management team. We had new land buying powers and new tools to get land into production and support more builders into the market. Behind the scenes, we were adopting a more commercial operating model and brought in land, risk, investment and real estate finance experts from across the private and public sectors.

We now have the skills and resources to get significantly more land ready for production, to create new long-term delivery partnerships, and to invest more public money to accelerate homebuilding and create a more resilient and diverse housing market. Over the next few years we expect to invest over £27bn, with a focus on ambitious regions with the greatest housing need.

Homes England is intentionally a much more assertive agency than its predecessor but our interventions are shaped and delivered through partnerships. We listen carefully to our partners in places and industry, create shared objectives and intervene to create sustainable changes in local markets. This is similar to the way City Hall engaged in London's Opportunity Areas, now with more levers to pull and real spending power.

Unlocking land

Turning underused public land into new homes and communities has been a government priority for as long as I can remember. But it has always been frustratingly difficult to achieve. Part of the problem has been that government departments only received the book value from a land sale. As a result, sites were released through gritted teeth and pushing through land disposal was not a top priority.

Today, Homes England agrees MOUs with public landowners based on shared risk, and a shared return of the full market value. We have the expertise to manage every aspect of the disposal, and we can ensure the site's full housing potential is realised through the sale. We handle everything from funding enabling infrastructure and remediation, to brokering land swap deals, to assembling tricky land parcels and helping rehouse commercial tenants. This model is incentivising and streamlining public land release, as well as capturing more of the value.

The market is certainly taking notice of our new partnership with the Defence Infrastructure Organisation (DIO) to develop land being released by the Ministry of Defence (MoD). The partnership combines the DIO's in-house expertise with the skills, people and finance of Homes England. Together we can unlock the constraints, create greater certainty and speed up home building.

Northstowe, in Cambridgeshire is a very good example of what can be achieved through this model. Homes England has worked closely with the MOD and local partners to maintain momentum behind plans to transform this former RAF airfield into a new town with 10,000 new homes. 45% of these properties will be Starter Homes with prices capped below market rates in perpetuity.

Together, we are clearing up this heavily contaminated site in phases and bringing high quality, development-ready land parcels to the market. The complex remediation process includes the safe disposal of unexploded bombs and many thousands of shell casings. We are creating a 1km long balancing lake to deal with the water table. These enabling works would be too much for any private sector partner to manage in isolation and can only be addressed through a long-term partnership approach.

We also focus on private land, targeting sites in the least affordable boroughs that are just too awkward, high risk or expensive for local authorities or developers to take on. Through our £1bn Land Assembly Fund, we acquire these stalled sites and progress them into delivery on a commercial basis. We work with local partners to ensure the terms of our sale support the local housing and growth agenda. Some plots are reserved for small builders and promote delivery through modern methods of construction (MMC), creating a secure pipeline for these important parts of the market.

In Burgess Hill for example, we acquired a strategic housing site which has been stalled for a decade due to complex ownerships and expensive infrastructure needs. Homes England will fund new roads and other enabling services, then break the site into plots and bring in developers with the capacity and track record to build at scale. The development will include a mix of 3,500 affordable and market homes, three badly needed schools and a range of leisure facilities. The package was shaped in partnership with Mid Sussex Council and carries strong local support.

Reshaping the market

A big part of Homes England's work is around supporting SME homebuilders and lifting the barriers which have gradually squeezed them out of the market over the last 30 or so years. We provide finance when commercial lenders will not, with a focus on supporting long-term growth within the sector and developing capacity in the MMC market.

We insist every grant application starts with a phone call, not a burdensome application process. If they meet our criteria, then we work with them to shape a funding proposal that delivers additional homes and a sustainable increase in their business capacity. Our investment teams, who have commercial backgrounds, maintain lasting relationships with our SME partners and look to add value and unlock more opportunities over time.

Step Place is one small builder to benefit from this approach. They struggled to access private finance but with our support have now developed a series of successful housing schemes across East Manchester. The workforce has grown from 3 to 11, and they are now taking on the regeneration of Wigan Pier on the Leeds and Liverpool Canal.

Homes England has announced several other notable commercial partnerships in just its first year of operation. A joint venture with Kier Living and Cross Keys Homes worth £42m will support the delivery of more than 5,400 homes. This was followed by a £1bn partnership with Barclays Bank to increase support for smaller and medium sized developers, complementing our partnership with Lloyds and our own Homes Building Fund.

In three waves to date, we have also announced a total of 23 strategic partnerships with housing associations, providing them with £1.7bn to deliver around 40,000 affordable home starts by March 2022. These long-term deals give housing associations the certainty to develop expansive, ambitious housing programmes, and the flexibility to leverage other sources of finance and embrace MMC delivery. As with all of our programmes, the focus is on encouraging innovation and growing sustainable capacity within the system.

Final thoughts

The skills I am using today are those that have served me well throughout my career in public service. I try to listen, find common cause and be very clear and open about what I want to achieve. I have been fortunate to work in organisations which are characterised by a clear sense of direction, a readiness to break with the ways of the past and a refusal to accept defeat.

I have enjoyed working with colleagues in all sectors who have been both forward-thinking and outward-looking. I have learned that successful council leaders do not rely on political orthodoxy. The best civic leaders are pragmatic problem-solvers. They know how to reach out to new partners and they are street-smart when it comes to making a deal.

We have all had to embrace new ways of working and build relationships with new partners. We have learnt more about how our different organisations operate. There is increasingly a shared commitment throughout the private and public sectors to removing the obstacles that stand in the way of new development and much-needed homes.

It is the same energy that is driving new approaches to succesful place-making. It is helping us all to understand more about how we can ensure that the new homes we deliver - and the services and facilities that go with them - can bring lasting benefits to the people who will live there.

THE VALUE OF PARTNERSHIP WORKING

DAME ALISON NIMMO DBE

DAME ALISON NIMMO DBE

Dame Alison joined The Crown Estate as CEO on 1st January 2012. The Estate's assets range from prime real estate in London's West End to the UK's seabed. In the financial year (2018/19) it had a capital value of £14.3bn and returned over £343m in profits to HM Treasury.

Alison worked on the London 2012 Games for over 8 years, originally as part of the bid team and then subsequently as Director of Design and Regeneration at the Olympic Delivery Authority (ODA). At the ODA she led on the overall design, planning and early delivery of most of the venues and the parklands for London's multi-award winning Olympic Park.

Previous roles have included: Chief Executive of Sheffield One and Project Director of Manchester Millennium – the team that spearheaded the rebuilding of the City Centre after the 1996 bomb. Her early career started in the Planning and Transport Department in Westminster City Council, followed by Chartered Surveyors Drivers Jonas (DJ) and KPMG.

She studied Town & Country Planning at Manchester University and was awarded the RTPI Gold Medal for outstanding achievement in 2014. Whilst working at DJ she studied at night to become a chartered surveyor with the College of Estate Management.

She was awarded a CBE for services to urban regeneration in 2004 and a DBE for public service and services to the Exchequer in 2019.

She is a Fellow of the Institute of Civil Engineers and an Honorary Fellow of the Royal Institute of British Architects (RIBA) and the College of Estate Management. Alison has an Honorary Degree from Sheffield Hallam University and an Outstanding Alumni Award from University of Manchester. In 2018 she was honoured as Property Week's Personality of the Year and inducted into its "Hall of Fame".

Alison is: a non-executive director of the Berkeley Group; a trustee of the UK Green Building Council; chair of the CBI's Economic Growth Board; and a council member of Imperial College and Chair of its White City Syndicate. Alison also enjoys coaching and mentoring a number of hugely talented young women.

There's an old African proverb that says *"if you want to go quickly, go alone. If you want to go far, go together"*.

The best examples of city planning and placemaking are done together, for the long term and with courage and vision. Cities and neighbourhoods are complex ecosystems with people at their hearts and this means that we approach regeneration with real humility, expertise, patience, and an open heart.

From time to time, of course, life throws complex and interesting challenges our way and sometimes we have to go quickly – to respond to some disaster (in the case of Manchester and the 1996 bomb) or indeed a huge opportunity (in the case of London and the 2012 Olympics).

My passion for cities and how we approach regeneration, reinvention, repair, and adaption has taken me the full length and breadth of the UK. I've been doing it now for over 30 years and I'm still learning. My fascination and passion is undiminished.

Indeed I still get hugely frustrated when I see bad city planning and bad buildings – these are not mistakes that can be easily erased or ignored. Real estate is real and leaves its ugly mark on a city when we get it wrong, for a generation or more. But when we get it right it is genuinely transformational.

Big or small?

The debate continues to rage around the "best" approach to city planning and placemaking. Over the years I have been inspired equally by Chicago and Daniel Burnham's challenge to "make no little plans; they have no magic to stir men's blood"; and the late great Jane Jacobs. In her seminal text "The Life and Death of Great American Cities" Jane Jacobs took on the (largely male) establishment, criticising them for ignoring "the most important role a city must play: as a platform for the countless little plans of countless people". She wrote of the immense diversity of cities and the density of street life, or as she evocatively called it – the "ballet of the sidewalk". It's a great question which I will return to later.

Public or private?

Many people have strong views about the public sector and the private sector and these are often shaped by their own experiences or maybe just influenced by lazy journalism. The truth is that there is the good, the bad and even the ugly, in both.

My deep roots are in the public sector, indeed, my first "proper" job was as a young and idealistic graduate planner in the Planning and Transport Department in Westminster City Council in 1986. It was during the era of Lady Shirley Porter and so my idealism soon hit the realities and fascinating twists and turns of local government politics and power. I realised pretty quickly that regulation and policy making wasn't for me, I wanted to be on the promotion side of city planning – shaping places and making things happen.

Since those early days: I've started, set up and led a number of companies, partnerships and businesses. I start with the principle that the best way to succeed is by combining the strengths of both the public and private sector.

The private sector can bring huge professionalism, expertise, focus and entrepreneurial flair, albeit that it can also, at times, seem very self-serving. The public sector brings a longer term, more purpose driven approach, serving its citizens' wider interests but more often these days (unfortunately) it just doesn't have the resources, powers and capacity to deliver.

Recognising the different strengths, skills and resources of the public and private sector and then finding a way to align these behind a common purpose or vision or plan is a hugely powerful way to build partnerships not just to get things done but importantly to get the right things done. And it goes without saying that the best partnerships communicate, genuinely engage and involve the communities in which they operate.

In the following pages I try to bring to life what a successful partnership looks like, with reference to my own, very personal, experiences in Manchester; London 2012 and The Crown Estate. I want to illustrate the very real scale of what can be achieved through partnership, alongside some of the key factors for success and, of course, the many challenges and pitfalls along the way. I also try to draw out the most important personal lessons that I have learnt.

But first I want to acknowledge that great people and great relationships make great partnerships. And these take time to build and develop and nurture and grow. The most successful cities and organisations build these relationships long before they need them. They know that the foundations of any successful relationship must include: shared purpose, mutual trust, integrity and the sharing of power.

Nowhere was this demonstrated more clearly to me than in Manchester in the days and weeks and months following the terrible City Centre bomb in 1996. And so let's first turn to the story of Manchester and how partnership helped the City to respond so quickly and so effectively, turning adversity into opportunity and hope.

Manchester

One sunny Sunday, 15th June 1996, the largest bomb ever detonated on mainland UK exploded in a lorry parked on Corporation Street, causing catastrophic damage. A square mile of the City Centre had to be cordoned off. Thankfully nobody died, albeit there were some awful injuries.

The ability of the City Council to get the City back on its feet and to have completely rebuilt the damaged core, in less than 4 years, was in no small part because it had well established strong relationships and partnership credentials with the private sector and government. When the City leaders needed to bring people together they already knew them and they knew what to do and how. This meant that super-quick progress could be made in setting up the dedicated taskforce (Manchester Millennium Ltd) to spearhead the rebuilding and to launch an ambitious vision/masterplan, supported by all the key landowners not just with words but with money and commitment.

At the time of the bomb I was working for KMPG and I remember taking the Metrolink through the damaged core and being so shocked, emotional and determined to do something to help. I persuaded my boss to "loan me" to the City Council (for 3 months!) and I went to see Howard Bernstein, then Deputy CEO of the City Council, and (somewhat boldly) told him I was the person to help him set up Manchester Millennium Ltd (MML) - the taskforce which spearheaded the regeneration.

Many months later, when Howard was promoted to CEO of the City Council, he gave me the keys to his office and told me I was now Project Director of MML. This was a huge vote of confidence in a young 30 year old and I was determined that I wouldn't let him down. This role allowed me a front row seat to see the power of purpose, combined with a serious delivery "machine".

The power and energy of a relatively small but completely committed team of people who got up every morning with just one intent – to not just rebuild what had been before, but to take the opportunity to replan Manchester's central core with an ambitious vision. This vision went beyond just a new and better mix of buildings and uses, to real placemaking i.e. new pedestrianised streets, gardens, squares and public spaces.

The Manchester difference is that the City combined this purpose with inspirational leadership with a delivery capability that was second to none. It re-organised itself and its governance to fit the task in hand rather than expecting the City rebuild to fit into "business as usual". The Town Hall came together with MML and specialist programme and project management expertise bringing a discipline, rigour and prioritisation that I'd never experienced before. These were difficult days, there is no denying that. It was tough and failure was NOT an option – there was so much at stake. But I absolutely loved it.

Howard Bernstein and Councillor Richard Leese, the City Council's CEO and Leader at the time, provided the inspirational leadership and proved a formidable double act that lasted for more than 20 years. MML was the principal vehicle to spearhead the rebuilding – it was a partnership of the public and private sector, chaired by a leading businessman – Sir Alan Cockshaw.

The relationship between MML and the City was seamless. The MML core executive team was a small one – just 13 of us, mainly on secondment from the City or Government Office or, in my case, the private sector (I was on loan from KPMG for 3 months which morphed into 4 years!). We brought a real mix of skills and expertise and set to work bidding for and securing a budget of £87milion for the rebuilding, using this to leverage many times that in private investment.

The whole City was mobilised behind the rebuilding – strongly supported by, and partially funded by, central government. The Cathedral was a key partner too, and I remember the masterplan, which the people of Manchester had helped to select, being blessed on the altar. That was a very real and spiritual signal of the City coming together to mend itself.

The key private partners were a small but critically important and influential group of landowners - M&S, Prudential (now M&G), P&O and Frogmore. These landowners had a long history with the City. Interestingly the City Council was a major landowner too and this provided important commercial leverage in the many negotiations. There was a lot of trust and respect and these landowners quickly backed the rebuilding plans – in truth realising that they could achieve so much more working in partnership with the City and each other than they could alone.

Regardless of whether you'd call that alignment or enlightened self-interest, it allowed the rebuilding to proceed at pace and pulled in significant private investment; signalling great confidence in the City at a fragile time. It was the era of out-of-town mega malls and there was a real worry that the Trafford Centre, being built just 6 miles away, could cause lasting damage to a weakened City Centre.

The Manchester story has a happy ending. From the rubble a beautiful new City Centre was born and the City's reputation for savvy leadership, partnership and getting things done went from strength to strength. As soon as the rebuilding work was complete the City focussed all its efforts on the next chapter of its history – hosting a hugely successful Commonwealth Games in 2002. Little did I know then that these Games would help pave the way for a later successful Olympic bid.

Suffice to say, Manchester changed the course of my career and influenced me deeply; indeed it still does. Of course, I never went back to KPMG, I stayed at MML till the job was done and then it was time to spread my wings and find a new adventure.

NEWLY CREATED EXCHANGE SQUARE, MANCHESTER CITY CENTRE   PHOTO COURTESY OF MARTHA SCHWARTZ PARTNERS

So what was the enduring lesson I learnt from Manchester? Howard taught me the power of purpose – doing something that you believe with a passion and that leadership is something that you do with people and not to them. And I experienced at first hand that people love to follow those with real passion, commitment and integrity. Howard started working at the City Council when he was 16 and we had this joke that if you cut him in half he'd have Manchester written inside him, like a stick of rock!

I still count Manchester as my adopted home city as I'd spent 4 very happy years there at university doing town planning, before spending 10 years in London and then finding myself back in the City working for KPMG. During my time in London I'd worked for Westminster City Council and for Drivers Jonas (DJ) - a private partnership where I also studied to become a chartered surveyor.

At DJ I'd written many urban regeneration reports and strategies as varied as Woolwich to Wales to Whitehaven. With the benefit of hindsight I felt that this apprenticeship had given me a really good grounding in how to work out the relative strengths and weaknesses of a place and its people, and to put together a clear vision and plan of action to deal with market or economic or institutional failure.

I also learned about the different models and the multi-various funding streams that were available back then (now sadly long since disappeared). I guess you could say that Manchester finished my (long) apprenticeship with a hugely challenging and hugely satisfying lesson in how to turn such visions and plans into delivery, or as I like to call it – the magic of how to get things done.

Immediately post Manchester I was asked to deliver a similar City Centre partnership and regeneration programme in Sheffield City Centre. This was the start of the first wave of what were to become an established model of Urban Regeneration Companies (URCs). Needless to say we took many of the lessons and principles from Manchester across the Pennines, to set up Sheffield One.

I rolled up my sleeves and got to work with Bob Kerslake – the CEO of the City Council at the time. He provided the inspirational leadership and commitment to partnership needed to bring the civic, community and business partners together to transform the City Centre.

I'm fast forwarding through Sheffield to my other two stories illustrating the power of public/private partnership in action. The first example is of London 2012 and the second is of The Crown Estate, an organisation I'm very proud to lead.

London 2012

The story of London 2012 has been told in many different ways, by many different people, through many different lenses, mainly because it is so compelling. I tell the story from my own unique perspective having been directly involved for 8 years; from the very early days of the bid (2003) to the end of 2011 when the venues were complete and we started the final count down to the Games.

It's a very powerful story of collaboration and partnership – literally one of a nation coming together to deliver the largest and most successful sporting event in the world. For me it was urban regeneration "on steroids". Our most important challenge was to create both a magnificent theatre for the Games but, as importantly, to create a lasting legacy – a new piece of city in London's East End.

London 2012 did not get off to an auspicious start. There was huge apathy and disagreement over whether we even wanted to host the Olympic Games in the first place. However the late Tessa Jowell MP somehow managed to persuade our then Prime Minister, Tony Blair, and the bid team was set up.

I recall it was a time when people were still hugely frustrated at the trials and tribulations and long delays of delivering Wembley as the national stadium. Indeed there was a bad joke around at the time that it was the only venue that we could be confident would be ready for 2012! In short we'd largely lost our confidence in our ability to deliver big public projects.

London had hosted the Games twice before, both times in west London and at short notice. This time the first Mayor of London - Ken Livingston - was determined it would be in East London to drive the much needed regeneration of a very deprived bit of the East End. The site selected was challenging, to say the least. The Olympic Park itself was 500 acres but add in the Village and Stratford (the site for the proposed new Westfield shopping centre) and it was double that.

I remember my first visit in 2003 of a polluted and derelict post-industrial landscape; a mere mile or two from the shiny new towers of Canary Wharf. I'd had a series of phone calls from Barbara Cassani (the Chair of London's bid team); she was clear that she needed me to bring some planning and regeneration skills to help with the bid. Somewhat reluctantly I agreed to help her, on a part time basis for 3 months.

Of course, when I first visited the site, I soon realised the scale of ambition and the opportunity to create a whole new piece of city.

But back then, two sets of powerlines marched down the valley, dominating the skyline. It was one of the most polluted sites in Europe, dissected by rivers, railways and roads. It was the capital's back yard – a bit of a dumping ground for an eclectic mix of uses, including: the Hackney dog track, bus garages, scrapyards, and the most famous local landmark – "fridge mountain" (i.e. a graveyard of dead fridges!).

Yet, the potential was obvious: a magnificent river and canal network, on the edge of the City of London, next to a strategic transport hub, and close to the creative and edgy parts of Hackney and a vibrant and diverse East End community. The challenge and opportunity to "mend" this tear in the city's fabric and to create a whole new piece of city – a brand new series of neighbourhoods nestled around stunning parklands and cleaned up waterways - was placemaking at scale. Our task was immense; we had to do all this whilst designing it to host the world's largest sporting event.

THE LOWER LEA VALLEY (LOOKING SOUTH)
BEFORE ITS OLYMPIC TRANSFORMATION

PHOTO COURTESY OF LONDON LEGACY
DEVELOPMENT CORPORATION

I was lucky enough to be part of the bid team in Singapore for the final vote on 6th July 2007; it was the longest day of my life! London had gambled big, taking some fantastic young talent as part of the final pitch and making such an emotionally charged presentation. I'm not sure there was a dry eye in the house – certainly all the Team GB presenters were in tears by the end, Royalty included!

It was an incredible moment when Jacques Rogge, the Head of the International Olympic Committee (IOC) opened the envelope and announced that London had beaten the favourite Paris and that the Games were "coming home". It was all a bit surreal seeing Ken Livingston (the then Mayor of London) hugging people like David Beckham! But from that fateful moment my job was to get the first plane home and get on with the job of setting up the Olympic Delivery Authority (ODA), the public body charged with delivering the core physical infrastructure for the Games.

Fast forward. First stop was HM Treasury. The undergrounding of the 13km of powerlines was absolutely on the critical path and we literally had a few short weeks to let the contract. We'd never done anything this complex before, against an almost impossible deadline, and the immediate challenge was to secure the £250m to pay for it. It would never have been possible without the collaboration, expertise and commitment of National Grid and EDF.

The scale, complexity and speed of the delivery (a 25 year development programme to be delivered in just 5 years) meant we had to do things differently and innovatively. We didn't have time to do things in a traditional and sequential way; this was a project with an absolute and immoveable deadline. We had to parallel and triple track. And we were literally starting from scratch. Partnership and collaboration was the only way this mega project had any hope of being delivered.

For the ODA the absolute first priority was to agree the brief with a (very) wide range of partners, and then a sensible budget that aligned with that scope. The project governance, decision-making and reporting also had to be clearly documented and disparate priorities and partners corralled behind a single plan. This was absolutely critical. There were so many players and so many promises made during the bid.

To have any chance of meeting what was the ultimate fixed deadline of the Olympic opening ceremony we needed the certainty of scope and budget and streamlined governance. There was a lot of wrangling and negotiation. We worked through quite significant changes to the bid and even with a lot of value engineering the final budget was a multiple of the original estimates.

The relationship and evolving deep partnership between the IOC, LOCOG (the organising committee), central government, the GLA and the ODA was fundamental to the ultimate success. An important early principle of cross party political support was an essential foundation and a commitment from everyone to joint accountability and responsibility for the success of the whole programme created a powerful framework to work out problems and differences "behind closed doors".

Strong relationships had been forged between a small but influential core of people during the bidding process; this deep well of trust and goodwill we knew would need to be drawn on many times during the lifetime of this incredibly complex project.

The Bid Book submitted as part of the bid process was the embodiment of all the promises that had been made and expected to be delivered. But of course there was a huge amount of work to turn these promises into detailed and costed plans capable of being delivered.

Alignment was essential in those early days to ensure that we had a clear plan for the whole project that everyone could buy into. London 2012 was set up as a single project, but in reality it was more like a relay race, with each one of the following 5 stages needing to be successfully delivered:

1. Assemble the land, demolition and relocations

2. Build one of the largest construction projects in Europe

3. Run two fantastic global events (the Olympic Games and the Paralympic Games), with the world watching

4. Deconstruct Games overlay and make good

5. Construct the Legacy – one of the largest regeneration projects in Europe

The role of local government, the Mayor of London and its agencies – principally Transport for London (TfL) and the London Development Agency (LDA) - were central too. The assembly of the site was one of the largest CPOs in Europe and was led by the LDA. Over 300 firms had to be relocated, as did 3 traveller sites; allotments; many businesses and a few residents. This wasn't easy and, in truth, the LDA team never got the credit they deserved. Assembling such a vast swathe of land into a single (public) ownership was fundamental to delivering the long term legacy vision.

The Olympic site straddled 4 different London Boroughs. Delivery had to be streamlined and the Olympic Act was passed on 1st April 2006. This established the ODA, with extensive powers and most importantly planning powers. Town planning was absolutely on our critical path for delivery. The planning committee, made up of a private sector chairwoman, independents and the 4 boroughs, met once a fortnight for 4 years and handled over 2,500 planning applications.

The ODA and the boroughs worked hard to engage the local community but in reality it was tough – for many locals the Olympics was a given and must have felt like a mega-project landing from space in their back garden. This wasn't helped when the required 12km security fence was erected round the site for the next 7 years!

During the bid process many governance and delivery models were reviewed – from public/private (PFI) led models to public sector led, which was where we ended up given a combination of risk, complexity and needing to have control of the programme. Those projects which were originally developer-led had to be rethought and restructured during the global financial crash, with the ODA having to take on greater cost, risk and responsibility for delivery, with private sector partners and investment flowing through much later, post Games. Three examples of this are: the Village; the IBC/MPC, and the stadium – all of which had their own particular challenges.

The other key challenge was to build the team. The charismatic and regeneration savvy David Higgins became CEO in January 2006. The appointment of the ODA's first Chairman and the Board – a heavyweight mix of public, private, business and civic leadership – followed quickly. Once the scope and budgets were agreed with HM Treasury, the Board were given a quite unprecedented level of autonomy to get on with the job of delivery. I became one of the ODA's 8 strong team of Directors, leading on Design and Regeneration.

Early on, the ODA procured a delivery partner to bring the private sector expertise, focus and capacity to help oversee and manage the design, procurement and construction of the Olympic Park. This included the decontamination of the site, main venues and infrastructure. The selected consortium was called CLM – a partnership of CH2M, Laing O'Rourke and MACE. The partnership between CLM and the ODA was a central factor in the successful delivery.

We soon realised that we had to invest a lot of energy and time in building this relationship and making sure our teams were aligned; time, money and quality were all essential to our success.

The strength of this relationship was tested to breaking point many times during the tough decisions that had to be made on scope, budgets and programme, as we navigated our way through the fallout from the global financial crash of 2008. During this period I held tightly onto the long term vision and legacy of the Olympic Park. I figured that this was the yardstick against which we would ultimately be measured.

The Olympic Park and venues were built by a committed team of over 30,000 people, from apprentices to some of the UK's leading main contractors, led by the ODA. LOCOG, under the steely leadership of Seb Coe and Paul Deighton as Chairman and CEO, delivered the most inspiring Olympics and Paralympic Games, with an army of the most amazing volunteers (as well as the actual army at the last minute!).

The Mayor's London Legacy Development Corporation (LLDC) led the transformation of the site post-Games to legacy, including the ongoing development and long term management and activation.

So what was the enduring lesson I learnt from London 2012? It has to be that success is a team game, in which culture and leadership are so important.

LONDON STADIUM, QUEEN ELIZABETH OLYMPIC PARK   PHOTO COURTESY OF LONDON LEGACY DEVELOPMENT CORPORATION

Ultimately London succeeded because of the talented and dedicated people who were trusted and given the space to deliver; mobilised and energised by a group of inspirational leaders - political, civic, public and private.

The consistency of the leadership of London 2012 was unprecedented in the recent history of the Games. That was the magic combination that delivered the best Games ever and an enduring legacy. Diverse organisations had to work together. We knew that we only had one chance to get it right and the only way to do that was as a team; or perhaps more accurately, a team of teams.

My last enduring memory of the Games is sitting in a packed stadium at the closing ceremony of the Paralympic Games on 9th September 2012. Finally, in that moment, I realised that I could breathe easily after 8 years.

Unbelievably we'd beaten the odds and delivered something very special – with the world watching. Our athletes had triumphed; we had new sporting heroes and heroines, Olympic and Paralympic. It was a moment of pride and happiness and hope for the future.

THE VELODROME   PHOTO COURTESY OF LONDON LEGACY DEVELOPMENT CORPORATION

The legacy of this special corner of London continues to take shape and I take every opportunity to go back there to walk, to swim, to cycle. Much as I love my velodrome, I think the real star of the show is the Queen Elizabeth Olympic Parklands – this is placemaking at its best.

We now come right up to date and end with my final story – The Crown Estate.

The Crown Estate

I started as CEO of The Crown Estate on 1st January 2012. Many people ask me how I got the job. The very boring answer is that I saw an advert in the Times and applied! I knew my finish date at the ODA and I needed to find myself a new role and I knew The Crown Estate from my early career working for Westminster City Council. It was an organisation I really admired; it owned some of the most fabulous assets and it was a business that had a strong set of values – commercialism, integrity and stewardship.

I didn't rate my chances much (they'd never had a female leader – ever!); but my nephew Ben was convinced it was meant to be, as at the time, I was living in Crown Apartments on Queen Elizabeth Street!

It was a very different challenge for someone used to setting up fixed-life public/private partnerships to deliver a specific programme. The Crown Estate counts its history not in years but in centuries. Its roots stretch all the way back to 1066 and William The Conqueror when all the land in the country was owned by the Monarch "in right of the Crown". These days of course, it's a thoroughly modern organisation. It's a public body, established by an Act of Parliament with a clear commercial mandate.

The business is led by a Board of Commissioners with all the power of an owner, running the business in accordance with best practice corporate governance. HM Treasury is our sponsoring Department and receives 100% of our profits (£343.5m in 2018/19). The relationship is a strong one, with Treasury respecting our independence and giving us the appropriate amount of freedom to run the business.

The Crown Estate manages a £14.3bn, high quality property portfolio. We are the largest landowner in the core West End of London and one of the largest owners of quality retail parks across the country. We also own the seabed out to 12 nautical miles where we've helped to unlock the largest offshore wind energy business in the world - a great example of partnership working with some of Europe's leading renewable energy companies.

We are a business with a purpose – *creating brilliant places through conscious commercialism*. This means that we pride ourselves in being place-makers and stewards – building well and building to last – investing in the public realm and the city fabric. We curate places, thinking hard about the mix of uses, the shops, the restaurants and places where people work.

Conscious commercialism is how we go about doing our business. It means taking care of the short, medium and long term commercial success of the business; but it also means that we care about the impact our decisions have on key stakeholders and communities and the environment. Our business values – commercialism, integrity and stewardship – are based on a deeply held belief that sustainability, responsibility and commercial success are intertwined.

We are a largely outsourced business and so collaboration and partnership is part of our DNA. The other unusual thing about The Crown Estate, given our commercial mandate, is that we are not allowed to borrow. This means that we need to find efficient ways to recycle money through the business. This has become critically important over the past 10 years as we've delivered the largest development and regeneration programme in our history.

We've used a number of partnership models to do this – for example we partnered with LandSec to deliver Westgate, an 800,000 sq.ft. new retail and leisure destination right in the heart of Oxford City Centre. It was a 50/50 partnership which allowed us to access the significant capital needed for such an ambitious scheme, share risk and secure the skills and expertise of the UK's best shopping centre development team.

However, the best example of partnership and how this has evolved (and indeed is still evolving) alongside our business is Regent Street. We pretty much own all of Regent Street and have done since it was fields on the edge of the City of London. As the name suggests this street was the inspiration of the Prince Regent (later to become George IV) to connect a large rural royal estate of 500 acres called Mary-le-bone Park (now Regent's Park) to his palace in St James's. It was a project of staggering vision and ambition and the Prince hired John Nash in 1809 to create this wonderful new street.

John Nash was arguably Britain's greatest ever town planner and working with his Royal patron was a powerful partnership. An Act was passed to allow the then Crown Estate to develop the street, compulsorily acquire land and to borrow £600,000 (a lot of money in those days!) to build it.

Regent Street was completed in 1826. It was the world's first purpose built street dedicated to retailing. Whilst the footprint stays true to John Nash's vision, the street you see today is not as it was. It was completely redeveloped in the 1920s and then again at the beginning of the millennium. It's an interesting lesson in adaptation as to how the street has evolved and changed over time, without losing any of its elegance, and its role as the UK's favourite "high street".

In the 20th century Regent Street was the place for fashion: hatters, bootmakers and jewellers. In the 1960's it was seriously hip and trendy (mentioned in the Kink's hit "dedicated follower of fashion"). But sadly by the 1980's tacky tartan tourist shops and airline booking offices were more the order of the day; the street was in the midst of a long and slow decline.

The story of the regeneration of Regent Street back to being one of the world's best known retail destinations is one of partnership. In 2002 many of the long leasehold interests along Regent Street's 2km of retail frontage were falling in and this brought with it the opportunity to take an active ownership role. The Crown Estate embarked on an ambitious new vision and long term strategy for the Street in partnership with Westminster City Council, TfL, Historic England, the Regent Street Association, and more recently the Mayor of London and the Greater London Authority (GLA).

REGENT STREET, LONDON

PHOTO COURTESY OF THE CROWN ESTATE

The real turning point was in 2011 when my predecessors signed a landmark strategic joint venture with Norges - the Norwegian government's sovereign wealth fund. This deal involved the sale of a 25% stake in Regent Street (a layered leasehold interest). We kept the freehold and the management of Regent Street but this deal released very significant capital for us to invest at scale and to accelerate our regeneration programme.

Needless to say we thought very carefully about the kind of partner we wanted and in Norges saw an organisation that shared our vision, values, ambition and was the ultimate patient investor. This partnership model, originally born out of necessity, has served us well and has now become an established part of our business model.

From a standing start in 2011 we are now working with a small number of exceptional global partners who have committed over £2.3bn to strategic joint ventures with us. An additional benefit of working with these partners has been to drive a deep professionalism and discipline to the way in which we report and run our business.

Ultimately good city planning isn't just about the buildings and the public realm i.e. the physical space. Increasingly it's about the mix of uses and density of activity – Jane Jacob's "ballet of the sidewalk" or the buzz of a place. The curation and stewardship of Regent Street and the collaboration and partnership with our customers and our community is central to what makes it so special. We do this in partnership with the New West End Company (NEWEC), the Regent Street Association and Westminster City Council. This includes a collaborative approach to marketing and operations, to our annual summer streets festival and local training, skills and employment programmes.

So what is the enduring lesson I have learnt from The Crown Estate?

It has to be that good city planning and investment is all about adaptability and stewardship for the long term. The world around us is changing fast and successful businesses find ways to keep evolving and thriving. Stewardship is a very powerful concept for me and one of our core values. The Crown Estate team seek to nurture and invest in our Central London estate so we can pass it on in better shape and with more potential than when we inherited it. In that sense, it echoes the philosophy of the Ephebic Oath sworn by the young men of ancient Athens to become citizens - *"We will transmit this city not only, not less, but greater, better and more beautiful than it was transmitted to us"*.

I would love to find a way to re-ignite this philosophy in all our great towns and cities.

DELIVERING INFRASTRUCTURE FOR CITIES

SIR JOHN ARMITT CBE

SIR JOHN ARMITT CBE

Sir John is Chairman of the National Express Group, City & Guilds Group, and the National Infrastructure Commission. Sir John is also on the Board of the Berkeley Group and Expo 2020.

In September 2013 Sir John published an independent review on long term infrastructure planning in the UK. The recommendations in the Armitt Review received widespread support and in large part have now been adopted by the current government, resulting in the National Infrastructure Commission.

Sir John studied Civil Engineering at Portsmouth College of Advance Technology from 1962-1966. After leaving John Laing plc in 1993, where Sir John had been Chairman of Laing's International and Civil Engineering divisions (and spent much of his career), he became Chief Executive of Union Railways. In 1997 he became Chief Executive of Costain, a position he held until 2001. Sir John was Chief Executive of Railtrack plc from 2001-2002, Chief Executive of Network Rail from 2002-2007, Chairman of the Olympic Delivery Authority from 2007-2014, Chairman of the Engineering and Physical Sciences Research Council from 2007-2012, a member of the Airports Commission from 2012-2015, a member of the Board of Transport for London from 2012-2016, and a Board member and later Chairman of the Thames Estuary 2050 Growth Commission from 2016-2018.

Sir John was President of the Institution of Civil Engineers from 2015-2016, he is a Fellow of the Royal Academy of Engineering, Institution of Civil Engineers and City and Guilds of London Institute and has received honorary doctorates from the universities of Birmingham, Imperial College London, Portsmouth, Reading and Warwick.

Sir John was awarded the CBE in 1996 for his contribution to the rail industry and received a knighthood in 2012 for services to engineering and construction.

Throughout history successful civilisations have recognised the importance of infrastructure in creating prosperous cities and sustaining a nation's productivity.

New settlers will put up shelter, administration buildings, rudimentary road ways. They will quickly have to deal with drainage and sewage, and obtain supplies of drinking water, if the residents are to have any chance of healthy survival. When the Romans chose the location of London; Peter the Great- St Petersburg, or Dutch settlers - New Amsterdam, New York, they would have all had in mind communications and access to the sea for goods and materials, their military defence and future trade. Their first activity would have been a landing stage or pier. In one form or another, establishing and maintaining infrastructure is essential.

The infrastructure that underpins our cities is designed and built by civil engineers. The water supply, the drainage, the docks, harbours, and transport systems. In the modern world electrical and mechanical engineers create the energy systems providing our electricity and heat, together with the most recent fields of telecommunications, broadband and digital systems. These are all referred to as physical infrastructure. Our civic buildings, hospitals, schools, are what we refer to as social infrastructure.

Today, cities can be great places to live, with excellent public transport systems, well-designed public spaces for leisure and social activities, and flourishing, well-connected businesses. They are also engines of economic growth. However as urban populations increase, many cities are becoming full and congested, the infrastructure on which they rely is under significant pressure, and this is inhibiting economic development and reducing quality of life. Infrastructure projects are a necessity in improving the lives of entire communities, increasing city's competitiveness and supporting economic growth long into the future.

Early career

I was attracted to a life-long career in infrastructure by the description in the professional charter of Civil Engineers; Harnessing the Resources of Nature for the Benefit of Mankind. Admittedly the promise of overseas travel and working out of doors were also very appealing. This was all despite preferring English and History to Maths and Physics.

The basic premise of designing and delivering infrastructure for people has inspired me for over 50 years in a career that has covered every aspect of infrastructure, economic and social, whether in cities or connecting them.

It all started in 1966, on a large social housing scheme in London.

Local authority housing at this time was building up to 200,000 units a year, whilst the private sector provided up to another 150,000. These large numbers enabled contractors to develop precast assembly models, primarily for the local authority market, with off-site facilities, high levels of repetition and speed of construction. Unit costs, however, were not that different to a traditional in-situ approach.

The system's nemesis arrived in the form of the Ronan Point tragedy in 1968. Four people died in a partial progressive collapse when a gas explosion in a kitchen on the 18th floor of a 22-storey tower block blew out an external wall. The cause was inadequate joint strength between the floor and wall units but the result was a loss of confidence in system building, which has only recently started to recover. Had this not been the case, the last 40 years could have witnessed a progressive improvement and development of off-site manufacture and a higher level of quality and productivity. Timber frame housing suffered a similar set back in the 1980's following a TV exposé of a particular housing development where there was particularly poor quality work.

Today, in various parts of the U.K., especially London and the South East, there is a significant shortage of affordable housing. It is not in the commercial interest of the private sector to overbuild to try and close the gap. If we are to recover to the number of completions achieved in the 1960's and 1970's it is hard to imagine how this will happen without a large-scale public housing programme. Such a programme would encourage the development of more system or modular building. There would be resultant benefits to the industry in the form of better productivity, lower costs and higher quality.

A few years later in the 1970's, I was working on major power station sites in Kent. These were oil fired, but one on the Isle of Grain, which was to be the largest in the U.K., had its underlying business case undermined by the dramatic increase in the price of oil. The result was a major increase in the use of gas in smaller, quicker and easier to build gas fired stations. A simple example of how, in the face of global events, we cannot always control the cost and nature of our infrastructure.

In London, we built a large multi storey car park near to the Tower of London. The foundations and structure assumed two tower blocks of student accommodation would be built on top of the five-storey car park. They were never built because they would overlook the historic Tower of London. As the client for both was the City of London, it is odd that they could not foresee this issue before they started to build, but it is a simple example of the regular objections to all types of infrastructure and how this can cause delays and increase costs. An issue I will return to later.

The ground floor of the car-park was double height, designed for large lorries. I cannot think of another enclosed lorry park in London and particularly in the City, but at the time the pool of London docks were still active, albeit on their last legs. A simple example of infrastructure which can take years to plan, design and build, is expected to typically last for 70 years but technology, markets and social behaviours may well make it redundant before its end of life whilst its existence prevents the rapid take up of new technology.

In another example, I worked in Poland in the mid-1970's building a very large PVC plant. The project was financed by Britain, America and Japan, whose technology, materials and labour were used in construction. By the time the plant was complete the bottom had dropped out of the PVC market due to over-supply and Poland was left with a large debt and no product sale to fund the debt.

Returning to England in 1978 I was asked to oversee an anti-nationalisation campaign on behalf of the construction industry. The Labour Party was proposing the nationalisation of the largest construction companies. The benefit was seen as bringing stability to the labour force by having two to three large regional public companies who would receive a steady stream of work from Government and the public utility companies. The expected September 1978 election was delayed until February 1979 and Labour dropped the idea. As with all marketing activity, you can never be sure whether your own contribution had an impact or not!

Through the 1980's I was responsible for highways, airports, hospitals, commercial buildings, and military establishments in the Middle East and Asia, as well as the U.K. The time to plan and procure these projects is often a reflection of the degree of democracy and influence of public voice. Construction periods are often quicker, especially in the Middle East due to a longer working week and the easy availability of cheap labour often from Asia. Hospitals, wherever they are built, can be the most complex and demanding. They are full of very technical systems and subject to the constantly changing demands of the medical profession who want the very latest equipment. Cost and time overruns are more, rather than, less likely.

One of the more interesting projects I was involved in came about in 1983 after the Falklands War. As a director at John Laing International we were, with our Joint Venture partners, appointed to build a new airfield at Mount Pleasant to reinforce the Island's defences, with no resources other than stone. Our first task was to create an offloading point which we did by anchoring the first ship to the shore and then berthing all the subsequent ships alongside it and off-loading across it onto a temporary bridge to the shore. We had to be creative in response to the lack of any road infrastructure and poor terrain.

I learnt from my early career that infrastructure comes in all shapes and sizes but its success rests on careful planning, innovation and an ability to be responsive to changing circumstances. Aligned to this is the need to ensure funding is in place and flexible to account for the risks associated with infrastructure delivery.

Funding infrastructure

My experience over the years of public and private sector ownership and delivery gave me an interest in the public/private interface in the provision of infrastructure. Traditionally, infrastructure was largely provided by the State with public money but there are many examples which, as a result of private investors seeking profit such as in Victorian Britain with our canals, railways and water supply, demonstrate how proactive delivery of infrastructure can be achieved. Also, private wealth put into trust for charitable activity would create schools and hospitals.

Not surprisingly Commonwealth countries developed in similar ways, others such as France, had more of a bias towards public investment and control. Changing technology has often made the investments high risk. Birmingham in the 18th and early 19th Centuries was the hub of Britain's rapidly expanding canal system, which supported the growth of our industrial cities in the Midlands and the North. Within 50 years from 1820 – 1870 they had been totally superseded by the new steam engines and railway network which was faster and on a much wider scale than the canals. In many cases, in a mania of investment, they could not recover their money due to the lack of passengers or goods, especially on a more local line.

Through the 20th Century the trend across the world was for infrastructure to be regarded as an essential element of a successful society and the physical wellbeing of its citizens, and so increasingly the responsibility of the State. In the past 50 years the pendulum has swung back as Governments struggle to find the capital needed to maintain and renew infrastructure. Inevitably Governments have turned to the private sector to own and operate the various transport systems and utilities such as water, telecoms and energy. This has been a particularly strong trend in the U.K. but is a contentious political issue.

Today the delivery of infrastructure will require a combination of public and private financing along with better understanding and evaluation of the costs and benefits of the options to provide greater certainty and clarity on value for money.

Innovation is important in how we fund infrastructure. In the late 1980's I had the opportunity to put together a joint venture to bid for a new crossing of the River Severn.

THE SECOND SEVERN CROSSING   PHOTO COURTESY OF HIGHWAYS ENGLAND

I consciously chose a French partner. We had worked with them before, building the natural gas network and then the first offshore oil platform in the North Sea. The difference between French contractors and British contractors is that the French are vertically integrated with design capabilities and the various specialist companies all under one roof. I was convinced that the capacity to bring design and construction capability together would give us the lowest cost for a new bridge and hence the lowest toll, which would appeal to Government. This proved to be the case, although the Department for Transport concerns that the French designers would struggle with British design codes meant I had to persuade them to join with a British consultant who also had a lot of bridge experience.

The Second Severn Crossing was an engineering triumph, by incentivising the designers we kept it within the tender estimate. We had been required as part of the deal to buy and operate the first Severn Bridge, where the tolls had been kept artificially low. So, we also took on the debt of £140 million from that bridge. Twenty years after opening, the cost of the new bridge and the debt of the first bridge had been recovered.

Recently the Government has lifted the tolls. I think this is a classic case of short-term politics, ignoring the need to fund long term maintenance and repair costs, which will increase as both bridges age and more money will have to be found from general taxation rather than the specific users of the bridge.

The importance of transport and connecting people

In 1993, after 27 years with John Laing, I decided to move on and set up my own consultancy. Three months later I had been persuaded to be the Chief Executive of a British Rail subsidiary - Union Railways, charged with delivering the Channel Tunnel Rail Link, a new high-speed line between the Channel Tunnel and London.

Over a two-year period, we finalised, from several options, a route with all the attendant public objections and concerns. Planning consent was through the Hybrid Bill process where Parliament approved the project route in principle and the Select Committees of The Commons and House of Lords listened to all the objections and particular local improvements demanded, and either rejected or accepted the demands. The same process has been used for High Speed 2. We then invited private sector proposals to take over the U.K. share of the Eurostar operation, use the revenue from this to support the financing of the new line and seek the balance of the costs from Government. In addition, the new owner would also have revenue from the train operators paying a track access charge to run domestic commuter services on the new line. In fact, these commuter services were central to the business case for this joint public/private investment in Britain's first new railway for 100 years.

Not for the first time, the private operators' forecast of the revenue they would receive, on the new Eurostar operation from Waterloo to Paris, was too optimistic. In particular, they underestimated the competition from the airlines and after the first year they had to go to Government and ask for help in order to finance the construction of the new line.

The new line terminates at St. Pancras next to King's Cross. The King's Cross area was run down with 105 acres of old disused railway and industrial land behind the King's Cross Station. St. Pancras Station, whose classic disused Victorian Hotel frontage was much loved, had to be remodelled and restored. The result is one of the best stations in the world, a classic combination of old and new.

In more recent years King's Cross has also been restored, its ugly 1960's appendages removed, and its underground connections improved. Most importantly, the old railway lands have been regenerated and now contain an exciting mix of housing, museums, art galleries, commercial spaces, restaurants and restored canals. From being an area to be avoided, it is now becoming one of the most desirable areas of London. A great example of how transport infrastructure can be the catalyst of much wider social regeneration in a city.

REGENERATED ST. PANCRAS INTERNATIONAL STATION   PHOTO COURTESY OF HS1

The Eurostar service to Paris and Brussels is now seen as the most effective way to make these journeys. Despite higher prices the commuter services are overflowing in peak hours having taken half an hour off the average journey between Kent and London. A key debate in agreeing the scope of the new line had been whether to have a station at Stratford in the East End of London. This station would only be five minutes from the terminus at St. Pancras, so it would to a degree reduce the capacity of the new line. It would also cost several hundred millions to build. However, the Stratford Railway land, the size of Hyde Park, was severely run down and ideally ripe for regeneration. Lord Heseltine, Deputy Prime Minister won the argument for a new station at Stratford. This station became a significant element in the case for London hosting the 2012 Olympic Games, which I will return to shortly.

In 1997, I was tempted back to construction, when Costain's shares were suspended and they wanted a new Chief Executive. Having handed most of my Union Railways team over to the project managers and designers for the new railway and having personally joined London and Continental Railways, the private sector promoter, I was getting bored. I think it is the case that we most often change our job due to dissatisfaction with the current one rather than the attraction of the new one. I also knew Costain would be tough but a different challenge.

Four years later the company was back on its feet, in profit and I had experienced more buildings and infrastructure delivery in the U.K. and overseas. Most notable was the Newbury Bypass, a cause celebre project which attracted Swampy and his protestors. The road, the A34, is the main freight route from the Midlands to Southampton. It ran through the middle of Newbury, so the town wanted the bypass, but the local villages were not so keen, and part of the new route ran through ancient woodlands. The bypass cost £105 million of which the cost of security and dealing with the protestors was nearly £25 million.

The decision by the Government to put Railtrack into Administration and the resignation of the Chief Executive meant a return to the Railways for me in 2001 as the Chief Executive of Railtrack, which was in administration and subsequently became the new 'not for dividend company', Network Rail.

Network Rail owns, maintains, improves and operates the U.K. rail infrastructure. Whilst only ten per cent of all our journeys are made by rail, the railway connects our towns and cities and every day carries millions of people to work in London and our other great cities. The major stations are dominant buildings in these cities and can either pull down or raise up the surrounding areas.

In my time at Network Rail we made major improvements to Manchester Piccadilly and Leeds stations and laid plans for the now completed development of Birmingham New Street, King's Cross and London Bridge stations. A visit to any of these active, bustling stations today speaks simply to the impact they have on the economic success of a city. Our railways are a constant subject of criticism and debate. Go to Germany, America and France, you will find similar criticism. Our fares are more expensive but that is a deliberate Government choice to place more of the cost on the user rather than the general taxpayer. Usage of the railways has grown steadily over the last 50 years, the fares would not seem to be too much of a deterrent.

Our main railways, or heavy rail as it is known, is, however, very expensive infrastructure and there are many questions to be asked as we try to get the right balance of transport modes in the future.

Infrastructure as a catalyst

In 2007 I stepped down from the hectic but deeply satisfying years at Network Rail and started my non-executive career as Chairman of the Olympic Delivery Authority (ODA).

London had been awarded the right to host the 2012 Olympic and Paralympic Games. Ken Livingstone had supported the bid led by Baroness Tessa Jowell and Lord Coe. Ken openly admitted he had no real interest in sport, but for him, hosting the Games provided a great regeneration opportunity at Stratford, in the East End. The existence of Lord Heseltine's new station at Stratford added to the accessibility of the area during the Games.

To turn 400 acres of industrial wasteland into an Olympic Park was going to be very expensive. National Grid pylons and overhead lines had to be dismantled and diverted underground in new tunnels. The River Lea had to be cleaned up, a million cubic metres of soil decontaminated and reused. Various businesses moved to new premises, new sites built for railway sidings and a new site built for travellers.

The total cost was estimated at £8.5 billion. You cannot spend that much money for six weeks of sport. There had to be a long-term legacy. So, from the outset what to build was dominated by the discussion: how does it work for the Games and how does it work as a legacy for London.

Fortunately, despite the 2008 financial crisis, an Australian shopping mall owner, Westfield stuck with their plan to build a 2 million sq. ft. mall on the edge of the Park.

The 3,000 apartments which were to be built for the athletes by the private sector were, however, a casualty of the crisis, so the apartments were built by the ODA using contingency in our budget and before the Games we had sold them on to a private sector housing company. Stadia and buildings were designed either as temporary or permanent structures depending on their legacy potential and the Park was designed to attract future development. The transport networks were improved. It had to be built on time and it was built within budget.

The commercial approach adopted for this major project was a series of separate contracts each with its ODA Client Sponsor. A design and build, target price, risk sharing, open book approach was used (NEC Target Price) which incentivised time and cost. A survey towards the completion of the works revealed that designers, contractors and suppliers thought it was the most collaborative project they had ever worked on. All the works were completed on time for £1 billion under budget and the contractors made a profit.

A similar level of collaboration took place at a political level. The Chair of the Olympic Board was the incumbent Department of Culture Media and Sport, Secretary of State, together with Opposition spokesmen and the Mayor of London. Both Government and Mayor of London changed political parties in the period, but the collaborative approach was maintained.

Transport improvements were made to the Docklands Light Railway, connecting it to the Stratford International Station and other improvements to the railway lines around Stratford Station.

In order to reduce congestion in London during the Games, large employers were encouraged to allow their staff a more flexible working day and major stores were required to concentrate their deliveries during the night. The International Olympic Committee (IOC) had always been concerned about the movement of athletes and officials around London, but in the event, with excellent management by Transport for London, everything went smoothly. Since 2012, freight deliveries have reverted to normal and with reduced road space to accommodate bicycle lanes, intense utility activities and the growth of taxi private hire, congestion has worsened, and average speeds reduced to below pre-congestion charge levels. In all cities this will be a major challenge over the next 30 years.

Post the Olympics, the Olympic Park has continued to develop with more housing, student accommodation, university buildings, cultural centres, and commercial development. The retained stadia are very successful and overall the London Games are seen as having delivered the best Olympic Legacy. London has a large new desirable place, enhancing the whole area.

It is worth dwelling for a moment on the approach taken to planning the Olympic Park. Five London Boroughs had land in the Park and normally would have had to give planning consent to any buildings and infrastructure. However, the ODA was given full planning power by an Act of Parliament.

To ensure local support, the ODA Chaired a Planning Committee which included representatives from each of the five boroughs. They were supported by planning officers paid for by the ODA but who operated independently of the ODA and to whom the ODA had to submit planning applications. Section 106 agreements were negotiated between the Committee and the ODA as normal. In the event of disagreement, the Chairman had the casting vote and an appeal could be made to the ODA Chair. This was never required. Since the Games the same approach has been maintained by the Olympic Park Legacy Company taking over the role of the ODA. It shows what can be achieved with a collaborative approach especially when time is of the essence.

Need for long term infrastructure planning

After the Games I was approached by Ed Balls, the then Shadow Chancellor, and asked if I would review whether the cross party collaboration we had seen in delivering the Olympics could be applied to an approach to long term infrastructure planning.

For this I was supported by Lord Adonis and a small team of volunteers with appropriate experience and administrative support from KPMG and legal advice from Pinsent Mason. Our conclusion was to recommend a statutory independent Infrastructure Commission that would make long term recommendations to the Government. In turn, it would be obliged to lay the recommendations it supported before Parliament for debate, with the final conclusions becoming policy, which could only be overturned by subsequent debate and vote.

Labour supported the proposal and said they would create such a Commission in the event they won the 2015 election. The Conservative Party kept their counsel. Labour did not win the election but in October 2015 George Osborne, the Chancellor, announced the Government would create a National Infrastructure Commission. Lord Adonis was the Chair, I took over from Lord Adonis in January 2018, having served as Deputy Chair.

The Commission is not a statutory body but an Independent Agency of Treasury. The members of the Commission are a mixture of economists, academics, engineers, industrialists and an architect, supported by up to 40 staff with an annual budget of £5-6 million.

It is required every five years to produce an assessment of England's economic infrastructure for the next 25-30 years, which supports economic growth, meets the Government's climate change obligations, and ensures sustainable socially beneficial infrastructure. Government is required to respond to the recommendations within a year explaining why it may disagree and its alternative intent. Public expenditure on infrastructure should be limited to 1.2% of GDP, this is currently about £28 billion. The private sector invests a similar amount in the utilities it owns.

The Commission published England's first National Infrastructure Assessment (NIA) in July 2018. The Government has stated its intention to respond in 2019 with the first ever National Infrastructure Strategy. In the meantime, Scotland and Wales have both established their own Commissions.

In addition to the NIA, since its formation, the Commission has produced six other reports at the Government's request. These have covered Crossrail 2 in London, the Connectivity of the Northern Cities, Smart Power, Data for the Public Good, the Oxford Milton Keynes Cambridge Arc, and Connected future on 5G development and applications. Later this year it will publish a report on Freight, particularly addressing its impact on Co2 emissions and congestion in cities. Government has accepted 42 of the 45 recommendations made in those reports.

Each year the Commission is required to publish a report covering the progress that Government has made in taking forward the recommendations it has accepted. Of the 45, 10 have been fulfilled to date.

Over the next year the Commission will start work on the next NIA to be published in 2023, but in the meantime has been asked by Government to produce reports on Infrastructure Resilience and Utility Regulation. It is 30-40 years since utility privatisation and clearly timely to consider whether it is achieving the right balance of encouraging innovation and investment whilst keeping down the costs to the consumers.

In the NIA, published last year (2018), its major recommendations were that our energy system should be 50% renewables by 2030 and could be 80% plus by 2050, at no extra cost to consumers than a system more dependent on nuclear. That we should have the infrastructure to support the change to electric vehicles with 100% of new car sales by 2030 being electric vehicles. That leakage from water networks should be cut by 50% by 2050 and extra capacity required, due to climate change and population growth, should be through regional water transfer schemes and extra reservoir capacity. That we should have a single approach to waste collection with full separation of food waste by 2025 and 75% of waste recycled by 2030, and the elimination where possible of PVC plastics. Broadband fibre should be available to all premises by 2033.

In addition, Government should allocate £43 billion of funding to our main cities through a five-year rolling allocation for spending by the cities on their infrastructure. The Government should commit funding by 2020 and the cities should have costed plans to present to Government by 2021.

This recommendation is in many ways the most radical. It seeks to reverse 50 years of steady centralisation by all Governments of infrastructure funding. It requires an acceleration and commitment by Government to devolution of funding. It will be a major task for the cities, and the NIC has selected five cities/city regions who it will work with to help develop their plans, which in turn can act as examples for other cities.

Cities face a cornucopia of challenges and opportunities over the next 25 years. Their growth is inevitable as countries everywhere urbanise.

Making our cities fit for everyone will mean new housing with the creation of places where people want to live with a strong sense of community. It will mean finding a balance between public transport, vehicle sharing and private autonomy whilst reducing congestion and carbon. Decisions risk being overtaken by fast moving technological change. High street retailers have to find a new role in light of the growth of online shopping. The regeneration of old industrial wasteland and waterways is essential.

All this can only be achieved by collaboration between the public and private sector, clear long-term policy direction from Government, clear governance structures and strong leadership, which seeks to achieve consensus together rather than the next change in ruling party meaning a reversal of policy. The commitment to producing a National Infrastructure Strategy for the UK is a first with the potential to be a great step forward.

Finally, we need to raise the quality of public debate about the importance of infrastructure. The professions of engineers, planners, architects, environmentalists and lawyers have a responsibility through continuous communication in plain language of the choices, the cost and the consequences of not delivering a core ingredient for successful cities and nations. Infrastructure is not for engineers, it is for the public. We have to make that our key objective.

HARNESSING
INSTITUTIONAL INVESTMENT

BILL HUGHES

BILL HUGHES

Bill is Head of Real Assets at Legal & General Investment Management (LGIM). Joining Legal & General in 2007, he has transformed Legal & General's UK property fund management business into an internationalising real assets platform. Bill's influence has a wide reach in the world of real assets, being recognised as a key player by his peers and often being sought out by Government and industry committees for his input on housing, infrastructure, regeneration and sustainability.

Bill graduated with a first degree in Economic Geography from the University of Edinburgh, and a Property Investment MSc at City University Business School. He is a member of the Institute of Investment Management and Research and is currently Chair of the Property Industry Alliance (PIA), bringing together the UK's leading property bodies to give them a stronger collective voice on issues such as policy, research and best practice.

The challenges for UK urban areas are increasing. With the majority of the UK's population now living in towns and cities, significant pressure is being placed on existing real estate, energy, transportation and social infrastructure. Strong house price growth over the past decade has made city living unaffordable for many, including workers vital to cities' health, education and emergency response services.

Air quality in urban locations is deteriorating and remains poor. Vehicle congestion, building concentration, poor design, and piecemeal heating and cooling installations have exacerbated urban microclimates. With the trend towards urbanisation set to continue alongside predicted population growth over the coming decade, these challenges will only intensify.

It is clear that there is an urgent need to improve and invest in UK cities. Some urban areas are responding to the challenges and putting plans in place for housing, jobs and infrastructure. There are huge opportunities across UK cities. Fundamentally cities need to adapt, change and innovate – providing the places and networks for growing communities to live, work and prosper. A future city should be sustainable, resilient and productive, and needs to focus on:

- Places (communities) – buildings and spaces that provide comfortable homes, productive workplaces and amenities for vibrant, healthy and socially cohesive communities.

- Networks (resilience) – the systems and networks that provide services and infrastructure adapted for an efficient and productive economy.

- Environment – sustainable use of land, environmental resources and adaptation to climate change. An efficient low carbon system, resourceful water usage, sustainable food production, waste avoidance, and recycling.

Institutional investment can play a key role in supporting this and delivering urban regeneration. By deploying capital in the most effective way it can support long-term productivity and prosperity. The needs are broad, they can span from efficient and low cost energy, to new jobs supported by work space developments, or providing a multitude of different housing tenures.

The importance of institutional investment

In contrast to the volatility and uncertainty of the current political backdrop, the characteristics of investing into the fabric of the UK can be structured to be predictable. Investing into Real Assets can bring stable long-term (10 + years) cash flows. They offer relative insulation from the business cycle, with the potential for growth secured against enduring assets that don't correlate directly with the economy. Real estate and infrastructure have strong liability-matching qualities which provide diversification from equities and publicly-rated credit for pension funds.

As direct investments, both property and infrastructure offer investors a high degree of control, with opportunities to actively manage assets to enhance values and cash flows. In a world where some investors pay handsomely for the ability to switch rapidly in and out of investments, for the patient capital of a pension fund manager, Real Assets offer attractively priced strong and stable returns. Banks also continue to reduce their appetite for long-term financing. Alongside increasing government indebtedness, we observed during the post global financial crisis dislocation, that this funding gap, which is increasing year-on-year, would present significant opportunities for institutional investors who have a track record for long-term investment into the UK built environment.

Personally, I have long had an interest in the role that investment plays in influencing positive outcomes for society. Having studied Economic Geography at the University of Edinburgh, I found a career in real estate and Real Assets provided the opportunity to materially influence the built environment in which society lives.

In January 2015, Legal & General launched a Regeneration Investment Organisation (RIO) partnership at No. 10 Downing Street in collaboration with Government. There had never been so much money available for investment into regeneration, but this was an important moment where the UK Government signalled that the future success for UK cities' regeneration would be through engaging private sector capital and expertise. It was also an important step for Legal & General as a business, providing a clear statement of our intent to invest in urban development. We also had the available capital to invest making the scale in which we could invest huge.

We committed to co-invest £1.5bn into RIO pipeline projects, alongside capital from other institutions and major overseas investors. This included working with the government's inward investment body, UKTI, with the goal of attracting an additional £15bn of investment into a range of regeneration projects to support UK growth.

The approach was focused on investing into UK city regions where there were many urban regeneration projects with the potential to unleash an urban renaissance. This presented a real opportunity for institutional investment to kick start major projects across the regions where infrastructure, housing and business opportunities had, for several decades, seen much less investment than in London.

This idea was supported by the then latest Office for National Statistics (ONS) data which showed that economic growth was rising at a higher rate in Birmingham, Manchester, Leeds, and Cardiff, than in central London. Workplace job growth in 2014 told a similar story, with lower increases recorded in the City of London and Westminster, than in Leeds, Birmingham, Edinburgh, and Glasgow.

Critically, the political landscape also supported this trend. The devolution of power to the city regions was gaining momentum, and Government had committed to investing in national infrastructure that links our cities. On top of that, the then Chancellor, George Osborne announced the formation of a non-political National Infrastructure Commission, to draw up proposals for HS3 ahead of the subsequent budget. He also used the announcement of devolution of business rates as the centrepiece of his speech at the Party conference in Manchester in October 2015. He called this "the biggest transfer of power to our local government in living memory", paving the way for local councils to encourage small businesses and retailers back into city centres. Rightly, the cities themselves were beginning to work together, rather than against each other, as well as articulating their own individual characteristics, competitive strengths, and potential to succeed on the global stage.

The case for Real Assets

It was clear that a new approach to investment was emerging where Real Assets, funded by private capital, would be an essential part of the future. We believed that this investment approach would unlock the best urban regeneration opportunities, whilst providing us with the opportunity to create high quality assets that we want to invest in for the long-term.

The connection between real estate and investment in infrastructure in the UK had historically been significantly underplayed. High on the political agenda, regeneration was identified by Government and industry alike as being one of the key drivers of UK growth, and a game-changer in retaining international economic competitiveness. It is here that the worlds of infrastructure and real estate most visibly collide. To treat them separately is not just short sighted, but deeply inefficient.

Skill set

The processes and disciplines used to underwrite real estate and infrastructure transactions have much in common. The need to appraise credit quality, assess and create legal structures, and consider a range of financing options, has proved central to delivering robust risk-adjusted returns. Where assets are used as collateral, an assessment of value and Value at Risk is essential. The scope to share expertise across research, investment solutions, legal and finance functions was advantageous. The operational benefits from one approach would, in turn, provide holistic solutions for the built environment.

It became clear to us that to effect large-scale change, there needed to be a joined up approach to Real Assets so that we could bring about transformational urban regeneration and economic growth. We had ambitions to unlock major urban regeneration opportunities across the UK – reshaping and transforming our urban landscape for the long-term. The piecemeal and sector-specific development of cities over past decades has locked in fragmented built environments and infrastructure that is poorly suited to changing social, economic and environmental needs.

Having established a strong and experienced real estate business over several decades, and with the knowledge that we had a small but growing Infrastructure Debt business positioned alongside Fixed Income, we joined the teams under the banner of LGIM Real Assets in 2016. This would allow the connection between real estate and infrastructure to be made, and critically it provided LGIM with the opportunity to engage in dialogues with cities about the totality of the built environment that is needed by society.

Making our money work

Large scale change requires patience and is not something that happens overnight. Despite this, we had a high level of conviction that this was the particular moment when the stars were aligned, and long-term capital – especially that sourced from pension funds – would be able to make a difference. At the same time, we believed we would be able to create large scale regeneration projects across the UK.

We developed an approach to urban regeneration which involves us accessing different sources of Legal & General's capital to unlock opportunities. The three components are:

- Initial direct investment through balance sheet capital to kick start key urban regeneration projects, alongside an explicit de-risking strategy.

- Creation of assets for direct investment in specific buildings by our Retirement's annuity funds to match long-term pension liabilities.

- Property and infrastructure expertise and development and asset management being provided by LGIM Real Assets, alongside the potential to bring in sources of Third Party Capital.

This combination of two sources of internally controlled capital with very different risk/return characteristics, with asset expertise, and additionally external capital can be highly impactful. By way of example, we are using all these components at our regeneration scheme at Cardiff Central Square.

Cardiff Central Square is a clear example of how our different sources of capital have transformed Cardiff city centre. It is testament to how our public-private alliance has successfully facilitated a major urban regeneration scheme. It also demonstrates how this approach is different to piecemeal development. Our approach has delivered large scale holistic change and has played an integral role in the transformation of this city.

Cardiff Central Square

In September 2015, Legal & General entered into a joint venture partnership with Rightacres (a local developer with an excellent track record and reputation) and Cardiff Council to bring forward Cardiff Central Square, a prime regeneration site in the heart of the city. Together, the partnership has enabled this scheme to be delivered, whilst stimulating real UK growth and reinventing Cardiff city centre.

INVESTING IN THE WIDER ECONOMY – BBC'S NEW HEAD QUARTERS AT CARDIFF CENTRAL SQUARE

The redevelopment is part of a five phase masterplan which will provide approximately 1.4m sq. ft. of prime mixed use accommodation, including a new headquarters for BBC Wales, and a Gross Development Value of over £450m. In August 2017, we completed the largest ever office leasing deal in Wales with the UK Government for new office space. With 750,000 sq. ft. of space either completed or underdevelopment, including Build To Rent residential, the scheme is set to create over 10,000 local jobs and drive significant economic growth.

Located in an excellent city centre location, next to the mainline train station, it was clear that this degenerated site could deliver major social and economic benefits, and could prove the model for the public and private sectors working together to change a city's future.

Legal & General Capital provided direct capital to give the initial momentum for the scheme. The BBC signing of a 20 year lease with five yearly RPI linked rent reviews allowed Legal & General Retirement's annuity funds to invest in financing the 150,000 sq. ft. building, and provided further belief in the successful future of the location. Local developer Rightacres and LGIM Real Assets provided on the ground market knowledge working hand in hand with Cardiff Council, demonstrating strong public sector engagement and the ability to secure strong leasing deals.

Collaboration and innovation are essential

Combining capital with a range of risk/return requirements, real estate expertise, positive credibility with Central and Local Government, and a long-term approach is a highly effective way to bring forward regeneration. With long-term investment capital this forces us to be much more future-focused with our developments, considering how our developments contribute to the existing community, and how we can create the widest benefits possible over the long-term. In part, this is about being able to demonstrate true alignment with Local Government, since we expect to be invested for decades. But it is also about having the desire and expertise to create assets that we would want to own.

It is essential to establish the right partnership model. This does not always mean just having one partner either. Some of the most innovative and successful partnerships can be borne from working with multiple partners.

By way of example, the English Cities Fund is a partnership between Legal & General, Homes England and Muse Developments, which brings together investment, regeneration expertise and long-term commitment to shape our towns and cities for the better. The complicated and long-term nature of these investments means that a trustful strong relationship and good governance are essential. As a long-term owner we have the flexibility to align our interests with partners to deliver on shared objectives through the life of our projects.

Whilst each partnership is different, the key themes which support their success are as follows:

- Shared vision

- Long-term investment horizon

- Capacity to derisk assets through operational knowledge

- Alignment of interests: sharing risk and sharing the upside

Concentrating on what's important – social value and the environment

Looking beyond the green credentials of a building through construction, we also need to consider the total impact an asset or a development could have throughout its lifecycle; from investment, throughout the design and construction process, to the impact of the building or development on its end users and surrounding communities. Taking a long-term commitment to urban regeneration projects provides the opportunity to make a significant impact on local communities, driving jobs and economic growth. A long-term funding stream can enable a fundamentally different type of community to be built which is sustainable for all demographics.

Unlike short-dated development models, long-term capital supports the acquisition of larger sites which can deliver the right type of homes and revive communities, working in partnership with the local area. It means we can make decisions for ten or twenty years, and account for future demand. Regeneration is also economically and socially useful, as is our deployment of long-term capital which will have a multiplier effect on economic growth and job creation whilst supporting local businesses and improving the quality of the built environment in a particular local area.

Through our long-term capital we have the opportunity to make a real difference, in the widest sense beyond the normally drawn financial impact. As an example, Legal & General's house building business has looked at how much social value it can create at Buckler's Park in Crowthorne, its new 250-acre housing community in Berkshire. This has been established by looking at three main areas:

- Utilising a Social Value Tool Kit – to monitor and communicate how much value Legal & General Homes have created to the benefit of the local community.

- Procurement – included a weighting on social capital creation on its tendering. On two contracts alone Legal & General Homes have created £2.895m of social value for the local community.

- Empowering Local Community – via the creation of a Social Value Charter. The Social Value Charter is a long-term up front, public commitment by a development investor to deliver positive community impact to the future population in a specific named place. It is measured in a total social value number in £s and by specifying the assets being created for the community's benefit. This is in addition to what development investors have to do through Section 106 and planning obligations and is a voluntary commitment to a community.

This approach highlights the importance of working with the local authority and being in a dialogue with stakeholders from the outset on how our investments could benefit the community. It is then possible for the community to be empowered to think about how it can benefit from our development activity. By embedding social value at an early stage, it is possible to help regenerate derelict urban areas to improve a community, bring more jobs to the local area, maximise land density and increase economic productivity. This is why it is important for all investors to think about the impact of their investment in its widest sense, whatever their timeframe might be.

As investors in Real Assets we have an opportunity to make a real difference, regenerating the UK landscape for the better and building healthy communities that we can be proud of. However, to do this we need to engage with local authorities from the outset and to let communities speak out. A different mind-set is required. This is much more than just building homes, new offices or a retail and leisure destination; it is about creating balanced communities within the built environment that are long-lasting and transformative.

This means recognising the need in an area and how our investments could help. An example of this is our £44.6m investment into affordable housing in Croydon through an innovative partnership with Croydon Council to provide 167 homes for homeless families. With waiting lists for UK affordable homes reaching over 1.3 million, and over 2,000 families requiring temporary accommodation in Croydon alone, the mixture of houses and apartments will provide much-needed stability for local families and residents, many of whom have been living in emergency accommodation.

The public-private partnership will mean a better outcome for Croydon families in housing need, as well as creating around £20 million in savings for the council. It further demonstrates our purpose to deliver inclusive capitalism, using our assets in an economically and socially useful way.

Delivering results and minimising risks – Newcastle Helix

It is clear that there is still work to be done on developing different models of public - private procurement. Policy needs to catch up with how development takes place on the ground, creating something much better, quicker and more predictable than going through OJEU (Official Journal of the European Union). This process can create wasteful costs, delays, and unpredictable outcomes for potential investors, and can be a brake on progress. It can mean sites never receive investment, or take decades to progress. Working with councils can mean that this procurement process can be simplified. The Helix in Newcastle is a good example of how a major UK urban regeneration site was progressed.

In December 2016, Legal & General announced a partnership with Newcastle City Council and Newcastle University to deliver Newcastle Helix, one of the largest urban regeneration projects of its kind in the UK.

In essence, this came about through Legal & General becoming an investor through buying into the land owned by Newcastle Council and Newcastle University at a fair price, thereby legitimately removing itself from the OJEU's focus upon goods and services. Sharing risk with partners we would like to work with, with complimentary agendas is also key to the projects we would choose to invest in.

The Newcastle Helix scheme is a good example of sharing risk across three parties. The transaction injected capital from Legal & General into a joint venture with Newcastle City Council and Newcastle University (the landowners) with the intention of creating a long-term partnership. The JV is responsible for masterplanning, phasing and ensuring delivery of each element of the site. The JV can draw down land from the existing owners, either to develop itself, or to transfer to third parties if appropriate.

The 24-acre science, technology and creative innovation community on a former brewery site, is located in Newcastle's city centre and is set to create over 4,000 jobs, 500,000 sq. ft. of office space, and up to 700 new homes. Legal & General Capital's initial £70m investment will deliver over 200,000 sq. ft. of Grade A office space, facilitating significant economic growth in the City, and acting as a catalyst for further investment in commercial and residential opportunities at Newcastle Helix.

The first phase of this innovative deal structure saw a sharing of risk and reward between Legal & General and Newcastle City Council. The Council is committing to a long lease of 100,000 sq. ft. office building which they will then sub-let to provide a visible start to the commercial phase of the scheme. Legal & General thereafter are developing a second speculative office phase of a further 100,000 sq. ft., designed flexibly to cater for evolving technology and occupier trends. Combined, these present the largest commitment to boosting the central Newcastle prime office supply in a generation.

LGIM Real Assets is the development manager appointed by the partnership. Since taking on the scheme in December 2016, LGIM Real Assets has been responsible for the procurement process from appointing the professional team, to managing the design and planning process, and tendering the main construction contract. Within 12 months of launching the partnership, planning permission was achieved for the first office building and a contractor was selected to carry out the development.

NEWCASTLE HELIX – THE ONLY CITY CENTRE QUARTER OF ITS KIND IN THE UK

The future

Forget Location, Location, Location – in order for our cities to become desirable places to live, work and prosper, we need Innovation, Innovation, Innovation. Whether this is in models of housing delivery, partnerships or financial structuring, we need to create new solutions to solve some of our most pressing challenges.

With both people and businesses demonstrating a tangible desire to reduce carbon footprints, a long-term vision, focused on sustainability, can also bring forward more energy efficient cities. These needs and necessary infrastructure should be considered in any city plan as a matter of urgency to ensure a focus upon creating an efficient low carbon energy system and a resourceful water usage system which will ensure waste avoidance and recycling.

As local authority budgets become ever more squeezed and the UK continues to fall substantially short of its target to build 300,000 new homes per year, more than ever we need progressive and meaningful partnerships to support successful communities. New ways of working between the public and private sector will be paramount to achieving the most successful outcomes for our future cities. Meaningful partnerships do not mean only working with local authorities but also working alongside institutions, like universities, which can be key to unlocking future growth in cities.

Of course, one size will not fit all and flexibility is key to establishing the right model. With the end of PF1 and PF2 we have the opportunity to create new innovative partnerships which can ensure aligned interests and the best outcome for our cities. As a long-term owner with a varied capital stream and risk profile, institutional investments can deliver this flexibility and ensure each partner's goals are met throughout the life of the projects.

Technology is advancing and being adopted at breakneck speed. As future cities become more connected, it is critical to have modern day digital infrastructure factored into city planning. This will create value now and in the future, representing the backbone of any city's transformation.

The historically sluggish nature at which real estate has embraced technological change has been astonishing. Growth opportunities are restricted by parochial methodologies, and the landscape has been littered with missed opportunities. So, the first step in moving forward is to recognise the need for change.

And change is here. The real estate sector has finally concluded that their systems are no longer fit for purpose and investment managers have sought alternatives to the archaic property management and creaking accounting systems that have been on life support for the past 30 years. The doors have been opened to the adoption of new technologies and digital roadmaps have become a talking point on the boardroom agenda.

Supporting a requirement to do and think differently, the real estate sector has seen a new wave of technological innovation. For investment managers, the smarter collection and interpretation of data is becoming critical in providing insights into business systems, customers, transactions, and placemaking. Harnessing the transformational power of technology alongside a more analogue human intelligence will allow us to better support this sector which must urgently change, identifying new business opportunities and potential unforeseen risks. Managed properly, big data can enable smarter decisions and support business growth.

Tech needs to become integrated in how we run businesses, not a separate entity. Like our Real Assets approach, tech needs to be viewed not as an "add-on" but as part of a city's strategy, with our priority on making investments that are focused on creating sustainable communities with good employment opportunities, high quality and varied housing in a digitally-connected and clean environment.

Conclusion

During these uncertain times, there is one thing we can be certain of; together - in collaborative partnership - we can achieve more for cities, and achieve more for the people and businesses who live and operate within them. Taking a long-term approach and uniting those that steward the nation's capital with those who curate place will be fundamental to success, helping to attract continued investment into the UK economy and making a positive social difference all across the country.

LINKING ARMS TO FIGHT RISK

MARC MOGULL

MARC MOGULL

Marc is the co-founder, Executive Chairman and Chief Investment Officer of Benson Elliot Capital Management.

Marc's track record in real estate investment and development spans twenty countries, covering equity and debt funding across a broad range of asset classes. During his 35-year career (30 years in Europe) Marc has structured and funded billions of pounds in commercial and residential developments, working with leading developers in the US and across Europe.

In addition to his role at Benson Elliot, Marc chairs the Bank of England Commercial Property Forum and is a Senior Fellow in the Land Economy faculty at the University of Cambridge. In 2014 he was the co-author of *A Vision for Real Estate Finance in the UK*, a landmark report prepared for the Bank of England which explored the relationship between commercial property financing and financial stability in the UK.

Marc is an Eminent Fellow of the Royal Institution of Chartered Surveyors, and a past Chairman of the Urban Land Institute in the UK. He was a co-creator of the Honor Chapman Memorial Lecture series, a focal point for women's leadership in the UK property industry. He is a founding member of the RICS Global Risk Management Forum and an adviser to the Ministry of Housing, Communities and Local Government (through the HCLG/BPF Commercial Property Forum).

Before founding Benson Elliot, Marc established and managed the private equity real estate platform at UK buyout firm Doughty Hanson & Co. A pioneer in Europe's emerging markets, Marc established the Property and Tourism team at the European Bank for Reconstruction and Development in 1993. Marc began his European career at Goldman Sachs, before which he was a Vice President with Chicago-based JMB Realty.

Marc holds a BS in Economics, *magna cum laude*, from the The Wharton School of the University of Pennsylvania, and an MBA, *summa cum laude*, from Northwestern University's Kellogg School of Management. He's married with three children, and his wife Kerstin – a Team GB age-group triathlete – has been Managing Director of Tate since 2014.

W e all have defining episodes in our lives: 'aha moments' when things suddenly become clear. I got woke (to borrow a term from my three twenty-somethings) on a spring evening in 1996, as I walked through Stari Grad (the old town) in Sarajevo, Bosnia and Herzegovina.

I was with a city official, an urbane, English fluent Bosniak woman, perhaps ten years older than me, who'd been at my side all day as we scouted possible sites for a hotel development. I was the Director of Property and Tourism at the European Bank for Reconstruction and Development (EBRD). Sarajevo had just been released from a three year siege following the Bosnian War, and I'd been given the Herculean task of organising a hotel development in a place that evinced images of Dante's Inferno. I'd arrived that morning on a United Nations flight from Zagreb, Croatia, landing at an airport surrounded by sandbags and soldiers.

SARAJEVO STREET SCENE AFTER THE SIEGE OF SARAJEVO, BOSNIA AND HERZEGOVINA (1992 - 1996)

Why a hotel development? The city needed to rebuild; it needed investment; it needed to become the administrative centre of a country stillborn in 1992 and subjected subsequently to a vicious civil war as ethnic forces tried to tear it apart. Three years of shelling (and sniping) had left hardly a window unshattered or a building undamaged. Every orifice of every inhabited building was covered in UNHCR plastic sheeting.

There was no guarantee that hostilities wouldn't erupt again, but there was a conviction that if the city didn't show tangible signs of recovery – and fast – the likelihood of a return to violence would be greater. Power grids needed to be rebuilt; services restored; roads and bridges repaired. It would take time, money and local determination, but all acknowledged that having a decent place to spend the night, for the hoped-for influx of foreign investors (and international development and aid agency workers) wouldn't hurt.

This was new for me. I'd been at the EBRD for three years, but it wasn't usually my team that blazed a trail in what we called 'early transition countries': certainly not in a war-ravaged locale like Sarajevo. That was left to the infrastructure teams, or perhaps banking. Most of my work had been in Russia, the rest of the former Comecon countries and the Baltics: markets where the private sector was emerging steadily after two generations behind the Iron Curtain, and needed commercial premises to support that growth. I'd funded office developments and restorations in Budapest and St. Petersburg; logistics in Warsaw and Moscow; hotels in Bucharest and Riga. It had been a productive time.

We walked and we walked. And as we walked, we talked. She told me about Sarajevo's history, and her vision for its future. She told me about the siege, and the husband she'd lost in the war. She was a life-long Sarejevan. She'd never worked in the public sector before, but had taken her job in city government in part because of her determination to make a difference, but in part because – in those early post-conflict days – there wasn't much of a functioning private sector in Bosnia.

I had spent my three years at the EBRD persuading private companies they could make a go of investing in our countries of operation, but this one struck me as a total no-hoper. In the dim evening light I couldn't see a future for Sarajevo, but I didn't need to, because she could. And she was offering to be my eyes, if I would bring my brains – my experience – and some muscle to the task.

My Bosniak friend understood three critically important things: 1) this was a challenge the private sector wouldn't have the courage to confront on its own (at least not in the timeframe needed); 2) the public sector had neither the skills nor the resources to take it on; and 3) if we couldn't engender trust amongst all involved – including three ethnic groups that a few months earlier were shooting at each other – we wouldn't get there.

NEVSKY PROSPEKT 25, ST. PETERSBURG, RUSSIA (1913)

NEVSKY PROSPEKT 25, ST. PETERSBURG, RUSSIA, POST-RESTORATION

ATHÉNÉE PALACE HOTEL, BUCHAREST, ROMANIA (1914)

ATHÉNÉE PALACE HILTON HOTEL, BUCHAREST, ROMANIA, POST-RESTORATION (1997)

For that local woman, at that moment, on that street, I was the most important person in the world. I had the power – as an experienced investment professional and a gatekeeper between the public and private sectors – to make a meaningful impact on people's lives. I had the power, if I was willing and able to use it.

In that moment, with that realisation, I was woke.

I left the EBRD before the Sarajevo project could be realised, but not entirely by choice. If I'm honest, I'd only joined the Bank in early 1993 because the UK property markets were dead, and the EBRD had the biggest chequebook in town. I'd come to the EBRD – indeed to Europe – via Goldman Sachs. That move, at the end of the 1980s, was an appeasement to my Swedish wife: we'd met at business school in Chicago, but she had little interest in building a life in the US.

I was a 'deal junkie' back then: obsessed by the buy side of the business. This was the apex of the 'Greed is Good' era, and my plan for Europe had been to carry on at Goldman Sachs as I had in the US – using the company's balance sheet to add notches to my deal belt.

But the Bank changed me. Maybe Europe changed me. Indeed, as my time at the EBRD wore on, particularly after Sarajevo, I started to think about making a career in public service. I was smitten by the impact I could have by bringing my experience, enthusiasm and energy (I was young then) to the public sector.

The fork in the road would come in 1997, when I was offered a promotion at the Bank that would have necessitated losing direct contact with the property sector. My mentor at the time – a senior executive at the Bank who'd also come from the private sector – could see the wheels turning in my head, and said: "Marc, this isn't your place. It's time for you to go back. With what you've learned here, you can have more impact on society from outside the Bank than inside. Your work here is done."

And so, after a billion dollars of development funding, across almost a dozen EBRD countries, I left. I built a career in private equity, enjoyed a measure of success, and spent more time than my colleagues and peers can sometimes understand engaged with the public sector, attempting to break down barriers, engender trust, and learn from each other: an effort, perhaps, to honour that Bosniak woman who'd lost her husband, survived the siege and would give her career to rebuilding Sarajevo.

I've had a few moments since then when I've felt I made a meaningful impact in the policy arena, but mostly it's been about small wins: moving the ball a little further down the field so someone else can pick it up and run with it. That's the way progress happens in the public sector: it's incremental (revolutionaries needn't apply). I seek out kindred spirits in public service: those who understand that neither the public nor the private sector can tackle the most vexing challenges alone, and who have the courage to take chances.

Just after the Global Financial Crisis I did a stint as UK chairman of the Urban Land Institute. That platform gave me the opportunity to meet some of the top local government talent in the UK. I used my American accent and typically American disregard for protocol to be a provocateur, to challenge convention, to float new ideas and encourage blue sky thinking. I would reflect often on a proverb that I'd heard during my time in Russia – "The tallest blade of grass is the first to be cut down" – and would think: "I'm willing to be that blade of grass".

Along the way I've formed views: convictions would be too strong a word. In fact, convictions tend to make me nervous, because too much conviction can get in the way of working together toward solutions. Conviction is the enemy of compromise. Five years trying to advance a do-gooder's agenda in the 'Wild East' had made me a committed pragmatist (and doesn't it seem right now that we have too many zealots and not enough pragmatists?).

Understanding risk

Some of my strongest views revolve around risk, the cost of capital, and urban development / regeneration: in particular, helping people who don't spend their days in the capital markets understand the importance of risk in determining the cost of capital, and the importance of the cost of capital in driving investment in – and viability of – development / regeneration projects.

But before diving into that one, let me take a step back. In 2012 I was appointed as a Senior Fellow in Land Economy at the University of Cambridge. Each year I teach a course in real estate development to a group of sixty or so of the smartest young people you'll ever encounter. They're our MPhils, and they come from all over the world.

My goal in the classroom is to challenge this group as much as they challenge me. I take them through various models of the development process and explain the key stakeholders (James Graaskamp's modelling of stakeholder interests remains, for me, the single most important graphic in understanding real estate development). I teach them about highest and best use, about planning and the basics of design, and equip them to carry out a proper feasibility analysis. And, of course, we cover project funding, delivery and sale.

Cambridge gives me sixteen hours to equip these young people to go out into the world and pursue property-related careers: eight weeks, two hours per week. I have to choose carefully how to fill those sixteen hours, and so there's some judgement – and an indication of prioritisation – in how I construct the course.

Each week's lecture has a title; most of them are pretty long (there's a lot of ground to cover). One lecture, however, has a very short title – one word, in fact. It's Week 2, and the title is 'Risk'. I spend two hours in a sixteen hour course talking just about risk, because the topic warrants that commitment. And believe me, when we're done, the students think so too.

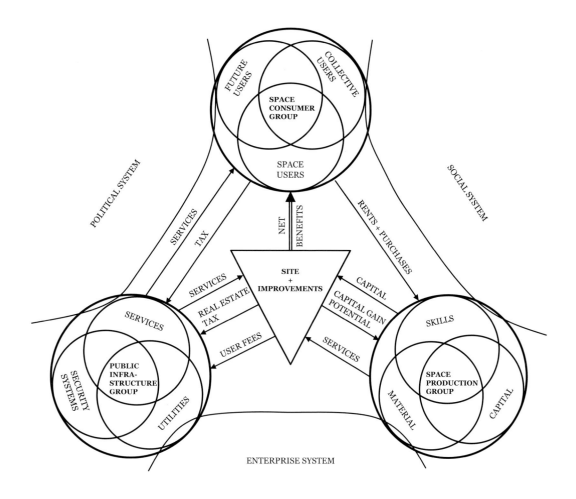

THE REAL ESTATE PROCESS, JAMES A. GRAASKAMP, FUNDAMENTALS OF REAL ESTATE DEVELOPMENT

Risk has a simple definition in statistics: it's the likelihood that an actual outcome will deviate from a forecast outcome. It's a measure of uncertainty. We use standard deviation to measure risk – the greater the standard deviation of a forecast outcome, the greater the risk. Most people are risk averse: they'd prefer a quiet and comfortable existence to a life of adventure. That's why funding development has always been a challenge: there's a lot more uncertainty in building a building than in buying one.

In a sense, risk is a tax, but it's an insidious tax. How so? It's a tax that everyone has to pay, and no one gets to collect. In a market economy, capital needs to be compensated for risk. That compensation takes the form of profit (of course profit is also a reward for foregoing current consumption in favour of saving or investment). As a society we've chosen to organise our economies this way because the lesson of history is that other systems of allocating capital don't deliver the greatest welfare to the greatest number of people.

We can differ about how the fruits of the system should be divided, and where state intervention is needed to operate or regulate markets, but, for the most part, developed societies have bought into the notion that a country's trade and industry should be controlled by private owners for profit, rather than by the state.

In the development arena, in urban regeneration (absent subsidy), profit drives project viability. How much profit? In economic theory, we would use the term 'normal profit'. By that we mean a profit that is consistent with the risk profile of the project: in an efficient market, it's the profit that someone bidding for the opportunity would expect to earn on his or her invested capital (capital that he / she is always free to deploy elsewhere).

In a market economy, 'normal profit' needs to be thought of as a project cost no different from any other cost. To make a project happen we need materials, we need labour, and we need profit. It's the cost of capital – the hurdle that a project must leap over (at least on paper) in order to be viable.

Development is a risky endeavour. That's just the way it is. And large-scale regeneration is an even riskier endeavour. Planning risk; funding risk; construction cost / timing risk; letting / sales risk – the list goes on. And to be clear, by planning risk I'm not just referring to 'outcome risks', i.e. the questions of what can be built – in scale and typology. There are also 'process risks': how long will the process take and what will it cost?

Development is also capital intensive, so the profit requirement on invested capital – the profit appropriate for the risk profile of any project – is likely to be a meaningful number. As such, figuring out how to mobilise capital for these complex, capital-intensive endeavours at the lowest cost (i.e. with the lowest profit requirement), should be in everyone's interest. And that's all about de-risking.

Mitigating risk

Actually, let me pause there for a moment. Why should the public sector concern itself with the risk profile / capital cost on privately funded projects? Two reasons: first, capital has a pyramid-shaped relationship with risk, by that I mean that the supply of low-risk capital (the bottom of the pyramid) is far higher than the supply of high-risk capital (the top of the pyramid). It's an oversimplification to say that investors seek to maximise returns. Were that the case, we'd see a lot more risk capital in the world, and we wouldn't see this pyramid shaped relationship with risk.

Investors seek to maximise *risk-adjusted* returns: the quantum of return for a given level of risk. And since most investors are by nature risk averse, we have the pyramid. It's why government bond markets are deeper than high yield bond markets; why banks can hoover up deposits whilst paying minimal rates of interest; why entrepreneurs perpetually struggle to get their new business ideas funded.

From the public sector perspective, the lower the risk of a project, the deeper the pool of possible investors. If we're fishing for funding (and communities are always in search of private investment), we want to cast our line in the pond with the most fish.

The second reason the public sector should be concerned with (and gain a better understanding of) project risk and profitability is more subtle – it revolves around the Section 106 regime (*Town and Country Planning Act 1990 (as amended)*), particularly the bits related to affordable housing. As set out in the TCPA, planning obligations are intended to make acceptable in planning terms development which would otherwise be unacceptable, i.e. to ensure that development is sustainable.

Some might argue affordable housing isn't essential to sustainability in the same way as road funding (to accommodate increased traffic flows), or the building of new schools (to accommodate increased student numbers), or the preservation of green spaces. It is, however, if one embraces the notion that sustainable communities – healthy communities – are diverse communities.

Without arguing the sustainable communities premise, I have to be clear that, as an economist by training (I took my university degree in economics), I'm not a fan of the Section 106 system as it applies to affordable housing. Put simply, it's hard to get an economist to love a system designed to stimulate the supply of a good (in this case affordable housing) by taxing the supplier.

This isn't just an economist's beef; many people question whether the Section 106 system is effective as a means of delivering the volumes of social housing this country needs. It's costly and complex to navigate and negotiate, it slows down the planning process and creates uncertainty (i.e. risk). It effectively links funding for affordable housing to market conditions, and it tends to reinforce spatial inequality through the viability system, since we can expect higher returns to be generated in higher value areas. In a November 2017 report, Shelter UK, the housing charity, put it quite bluntly: "The use of viability assessments leads to the undersupply of affordable housing".

If we as a society decide that affordable housing is an essential common good, and market mechanisms are not supplying that good, then the public sector should step in and provide appropriate funding via the public purse (and yes, have the courage to raise taxes, if necessary, to pay for it). Delivery mechanics are a second order issue.

We don't wait for the private sector to deliver roads, schools or hospitals, even if we have mechanisms, like the Section 106 regime, to mitigate the impact of new development on these public resources, so why do we allow an essential need like housing to be held hostage to market conditions? And as long as we rely on an affordable housing delivery model that's constructed on the backs of a market housing system, I fear the supply of affordable housing will always be harpooned, Ahab-like, to the white whale of project viability.

But as an industry we have to play the cards we've been dealt, and that includes the Section 106 card – with nothing getting built if it's not viable (in policy and investment market terms). And investment viability presumes an adequate risk-adjusted return on capital (i.e. a normal profit).

If one takes the expected end value and delivery costs for any development project (excluding Section 106) as a given, then the relationship between risk and Section 106 should be clear (at least for projects on the cusp of assessment viability for affordable housing contributions). For every pound we can take down the required profit on a project (by de-risking), that's an extra pound that could be available for affordable housing.

The government's *Planning Practice Guidance for Viability* (May 2019) makes quite prominent the relationship between risk mitigation and affordable housing. The guidance states: "For the purpose of plan making an assumption of 15-20% of gross development value (GDV) may be considered a suitable return to developers in order to establish the viability of plan policies". However, the guidance goes on to state: "Plan makers may choose to apply alternative figures where there is evidence to support this according to the type, scale *and risk profile* of planned development", (emphasis added).

In short, the lower the development risk, the lower the required profit. **Q.E.D.**

Developers think risk mitigation day-in and day-out. Partly that's driven by the joint challenges of sourcing capital and making projects viable. Ultimately, though, it's driven by an even more basic self-interest: the goal of maximising risk-adjusted returns.

Yet, it's not often enough that I hear planners and other local officials talk about risk measurement and risk mitigation. Reducing developer profit requirements – as a route to a more significant Section 106 contribution – I hear about a lot. If only the developer were 'appropriately motivated' and would skinny down their profit margin (based on a sense of *noblesse oblige*?). Or could bring in a domestic institution with 'long-term capital' (translation: cheap capital). Or, failing those two options, one can hope for the mythical Asian investor 'who just looks at these things differently'.

All of these are possible. They happen from time to time. But they're not a realistic basis on which to advance the volume of projects we need to resolve the UK housing crisis or to underpin regeneration efforts across this country. If we carry on as we are, we'll constantly find ourselves 'viability challenged', engaged in long, heated arguments about 'fair' Section 106 contributions, with projects stuck on the drawing board. 'Cheap capital' is fundamentally not risk-seeking, and risk capital is rarely cheap.

Developers mitigate construction risk through fixed-price contracts; interest rate risk through hedging; letting and sales risk through pre-letting or pre-sales. All too often, though, it's the entitlement risks associated with development – the engagements with local authorities and local activists – that are the most vexing for developers, and the most off-putting for the investors that fund their projects.

Why? Because every project is different, every local authority's attitude toward development is different and every planning process and planning professional is different. That wouldn't matter if there were 'rules' for development chiseled on a couple of tablets brought down from a mountain, but there aren't. Our planning system in the UK is by design less than fully prescriptive, so those we entrust with shaping our cities can operate dynamically in a world that outpaces even the most dedicated politician or plan-maker.

And it isn't just planning issues where private sector sponsors find themselves negotiating with local government during the development process. Big chunks of our city and town centres have been built on council-controlled land, granted in the past to developers by way of long leaseholds. These leaseholds frequently need to be restructured to accommodate re-development, and the posture taken by the local government negotiating team can make or break a project. Resolution of rights of light issues (use of Section 237 powers) and compulsory purchase decisions (Section 226 powers) are other areas where engagement with local officials can be essential, but the uncertainty surrounding timing and outcome can be significant.

And to be clear, there is a cost of time. In the finance world, the cost of capital is generally expressed as an annualised return requirement (internal rate of return), not as a static measure (like development profit % of GDV). IRR is a time-driven measure, akin to an APR on a mortgage, or a yield-to-maturity on a bond. Pushing back the point at which a project can be brought into use and made cash flow generative can have an enormous impact on investor returns. An extra year spent toing and froing with a planning department or development agency could easily equate to a 20% erosion in development profit. Time really is money in a world where investment knows no borders.

Alastair Ross Goobey, the legendary British investment manager, used to speak of four essential risks in property development: planning, funding, delivery and market. His view was that you could control the second by having sensible arrangements, the third by having the best people, and the fourth by careful choice of location and timing. It was the first of the four risks – planning – that worried Ross Goobey the most; it was the one he felt least able to control. For him, as for many institutional investors, it was a risk best avoided.

But entitlement (and related) risks can be mitigated, and indeed must be mitigated, if we wish to transform our communities – to make them fit for purpose in a changing world. We need to de-risk the delivery process if we wish to mobilise more capital – cheaper capital – for the task. Nobody wants to see high streets devoid of life because retail space designed decades ago is unsuitable for today's requirements, or walk past the brooding hulks of empty buildings that will never see use as office space again because they're functionally obsolete. Our built environment needs to change, and our people and processes need to support that change.

Planning officers, economic development professionals and the like are on the front lines of community development and regeneration. The best bring a missionary zeal to their work that is often the first step in turning ideas into reality. Yes, they may have to lock horns with the development industry along the way (local officials have a broad array of stakeholder interests to represent) but that doesn't preclude active engagement in, and support for, projects they believe in. I've seen it in many locales, not least in Birmingham.

Making it happen

I saw it quite recently in London, on the occasion of this year's end-of-term field trip for my Cambridge class. Each year the class spends a day touring and learning about one of London's most trailblazing development projects. Amongst others, we've visited Television Centre (Stanhope), St James's Market (The Crown Estate), Nova (Landsec) and King's Cross (Argent). This year we were the guests of Lipton Rogers and Sir Stuart Lipton, the iconoclastic developer of Broadgate and Chiswick Park and, more recently, London's 22 Bishopsgate.

22 BISHOPSGATE (TWENTYTWO), LONDON

When completed next year, TwentyTwo will be the tallest building in the City of London. TwentyTwo will also be notable for being the first building in the UK to earn a certification from the WELL Building Institute, an organisation that has moved beyond the environmental impact of buildings to consider how those same buildings "improve health and well-being for everyone that visits, works in or experiences" them. WELL is about more than sustainability: it's about people and communities ('collective users' to borrow James Graaskamp's term).

As part of the line-up of speakers, Sir Stuart had invited Gwyn Richards, head of design within the City of London's planning office, to present. As is his way, Sir Stuart punctuated Gwyn's presentation with his own running commentary, until Gwyn's planned solo became a duet. What was eminently clear to anyone listening to these two was the respect each had for the other, the commonality of vision (presumably developed over an extended period of time working together), and the depth of understanding of each side's objectives and needs.

Unlike many of the other tower buildings in the City, with their articulated designs and catchy nicknames, TwentyTwo is simple in its shape: in the words of the *Evening Standard*, a building that "lacks architectural flair"; less flatteringly, it's "an eighty metre wide hulk" (*The Guardian*). Love it or hate it, TwentyTwo is a building of its time: conceived and commenced without a pre-let, amidst the uncertainty of the Brexit referendum, design efficiency was probably essential in driving investment viability.

Funding mega projects like TwentyTwo is never easy; funding something of that scale in 2016 might have been impossible if Sir Stuart couldn't persuade his institutional backers that the risks involved were measurable and manageable, including the risk of design approval. To do that, he had to have confidence that the City of London planning team would approach the endeavour as a shared challenge, rather than as an adversarial confrontation, bringing the necessary clarity, commerciality and courage to the task.

It worked because the City's team understood the challenges Sir Stuart's team was facing, but it also worked because the planners recognised they too had an interest in a successful outcome: ensuring the City's office supply pipeline would keep moving during an uncertain time. The rest may be tea leaf reading, but I suspect if 'making it happen' meant foregoing a Cheesegrater, a Gherkin or a Walkie-Talkie – if it meant risking a measure of design opprobrium to bring online a healthy workplace for 12,000 people – then that was a risk the City's team was willing to take.

One luxury of the civil service, of course, is you don't have to face voters (or shareholders). That's a good thing. Just like in my role at the EBRD, one can focus on societal or community impact, and a broader (and often longer term) set of developmental objectives, without the constant sniping and social media abuse that politicians and prominent business leaders have to deal with.

CITY OF LONDON SKYLINE, SPRING 2019

Still, it takes courage to be a risk taker in the public sector, as the reward systems don't encourage risk-taking. The best planning officers I've come across are those who dare to challenge convention, who will engage vocal minorities in support of a silent majority, and who recognise that it's down to them to defend the voiceless (including those without housing, and thus without a vote) against the vociferous. The best public servants – whatever their role – are willing to be the tallest blade of grass, knowing someday they might be cut down. With over twenty years of public service between myself and my wife, we know it can be a thankless calling.

For planners, the job isn't made easier by the reality that they have no formal powers within the planning system (unless delegated). Those powers appropriately reside with elected officials. But I had no formal authority at the EBRD either: power was vested in the Bank's Board of Directors. Over time, though, I gained my board's trust and respect, and never once did I have a recommendation turned down. Also, there is a terrible staffing shortage in the UK planning arena and too many planners are consequently overburdened. Planning departments have been hollowed out in recent years (often with the most experienced planners departing), victims of cost-costing amongst local governments.

Finally, there is a skills deficiency in many UK planning departments, not least in the commercial aspects of development. Few planning departments can bring to bear on a project the resources and talent available to the City of London, and that's a handicap in any commercial negotiation. At one level, this can expose our communities to developers exploiting the viability system due to a knowledge advantage; at another level it can lead to paralysis or unreasonable asks from those doing their best to represent the community's interests.

Does the answer to the skills gap issue lie in bringing private sector-trained professionals into local government agencies? Perhaps, but not necessarily. Whilst that orientation and those business skills can be helpful, private sector training and experience revolves around maximising one's own financial position, rather than juggling a range of stakeholder interests and developmental goals. These might relate to community development, delivery of social housing, growing the tax base, lowering crime rates or delivering better health outcomes: not all are easily quantified.

I saw this at the EBRD, where professionals trained in the private sector (myself included) often had to be 're-programmed': taught to shift their analytical framework from a narrow (and sometimes overly aggressive) focus on financial returns, to a broader focus on the full range of economic benefits potential projects could deliver. We had to be 'doers': we had to find a way to make projects work, balancing the financial objectives of our project sponsors with the broader economic interests of our host countries. That's the essential challenge of development banking: the private sector can always walk from a deal (money is mobile), but communities need growth and renewal, and, in that sense, have to create an environment that captivates (captures?) capital and makes deals happen.

So yes, ideally it would be better if we could deepen the commercial understanding of our planning officials, but, even without finance degrees or MPhils in Land Economy, plenty of planners and other local development officials have the experience, instincts and institutional knowledge to advise and guide the protagonists in the development process, whilst protecting the positions of those they represent. Great planners have a vision of how communities should evolve, and can play a crucial role in imparting that vision to developers and the elected officials who hold the power to decide on planning applications.

But it is essential that our planners and development officials understand – and embrace – the importance of risk mitigation as a tool to achieving their own and their communities' goals. They need to be risk slayers, and they need to measure themselves as such. This isn't about rolling over: it's about doing everything possible to drive uncertainty out of development appraisals, as a route to reducing the cost of capital and resulting profit requirements. That's the route to tapping into lower cost capital, tapping into *more* capital, and advancing the regeneration agenda.

No one in the development process benefits from risk: for the developer it increases the cost of capital, making it harder to source funding and assemble viable projects; for the risk-averse investor it reduces the appeal of any proposed project; for the public sector – and for society more broadly – it raises the viability bar and ultimately reduces the supply of affordable housing and slows economic development.

The alternative to all of this, in pursuit of planning predictability and consequent risk reduction, would be to make the process more prescriptive: to codify more, and empower our civil servants less. But would we want that? As the world moves faster, would we want to embrace a system that could or should only move slower? I can't imagine that. I've seen such systems on the Continent, and they don't work as well as our UK planning system.

So, if we wish to sustain the suppleness of our system, and still meet the needs of all who engage with it, we're dependant on the civil servants who administer the system to provide the clarity and confidence that developers and their funders seek, and to make it work for all of us. Our planners need to be active partners in the development process, sharing the urgency and risk obsession of their private sector brethren.

Leaving Sarajevo

After an overnight stay in a local guest house, I left Sarajevo by car (there were no UN flights that day). The route out was via Split, on the Croatian coast. The road to Split passed through the Bosnian city of Mostar, the most bombed city in the war, and one where Croat forces would still take periodic pot shots from the hillside. Many people remember Mostar because of a centuries old bridge in the centre of town, built by the Ottomans, that had been needlessly destroyed in the war.

The few cars approaching Mostar from the east would be marshalled by Swedish peacekeepers who controlled the area east of the city. The soldiers would sit on their armoured personnel carriers, guns at the ready, until three cars were ready to cross the city. A soldier would take the wheel of each car, and we were instructed to lie down in the back seat. An armoured personnel carrier would lead the mini convoy through Mostar, with another trailing.

As I waited for the convoy to assemble, I chatted with one of the Swedish soldiers (yes, I was nervous). He appreciated that I could speak passable Swedish, and took a liking to me. When it was time to move, he said, "We're going to put you behind the beer truck: they never shoot at the beer truck." I was still nervous. He linked arms with me, walked me to the car, and showed me how to 'get small' in the back seat. I passed through Mostar without incident.

STARI MOST, MOSTAR, BOSNIA AND HERZEGOVINA

A lifelong lesson in effective risk management (stay behind the beer truck), an appropriate coda to my work in Sarajevo, and a useful metaphor – linking arms – for making an imperfect UK planning system work that little bit better for everyone.

Development and regeneration will always be contentious, there are too many interests to reconcile for it to be otherwise. There is, however, a common enemy: risk. If we want to make even a small dent in the chronic shortage of affordable housing in this country, if we want to advance regeneration and economic development in other ways, the public and private sectors must link arms and fight that enemy together.